# THE MONEY-BOX

THE
# MONEY-BOX
BY
*ROBERT LYND*

*Essay Index Reprint Series*

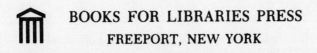

**BOOKS FOR LIBRARIES PRESS**
FREEPORT, NEW YORK

First Published 1926
Reprinted 1969

STANDARD BOOK NUMBER:
8369-1091-5


LIBRARY OF CONGRESS CATALOG CARD NUMBER:
70-84321


PRINTED IN THE UNITED STATES OF AMERICA

TO
ROBBIE LOWRY

# CONTENTS

## CONTENTS

# THE MONEY-BOX

# THE MONEY-BOX

## The Money-Box

THE elder of my nieces had brought home a money-box from the Christmas tree at a party. It was a charming thing made in the shape of a house, with long windows painted on the front. "How does one open it?" she asked me, turning it upside down, and tugging at floor, gable-ends and roof in turn in the hope that something would give way. "Yes," I said, taking it from her and examining it, "that *is* the important thing to know about a money-box." "No child," continued my niece, taking it back and shaking it vigorously, "ever put more than twopence into a money-box, unless she knew how to open it." "Do children still have money-boxes? What about the children at school?" I asked her. "Oh, yes," she said, "but they all know how to open them, or they know how to get the money out with screwdrivers and things. Belinda's always having money-boxes given to her— mostly those ones in the shape of letter-boxes—but, as soon as she has saved twopence, she sees a toffee-apple in a shop and wants them back again. So, of course, she has to break the money-box open. You can easily get the bottom off that kind of money-

box with a tin-opener." "But the money-box," I
protested, "probably costs at least sixpence. Isn't
it rather an expensive way of getting out twopence?" "Oh, *she* didn't buy the money-box."
"No," I agreed, "one has to remember that."
"Then," my niece went on, "there's the sort of
money-box that nobody's supposed to be able to
open, but that bursts open when it's full. Some
kind of spring or other. Of course, the children
have to stuff them with all kinds of things when
they want their money back. It's quite easy. Anything does as long as it makes the spring work."
Just then, as if by a miracle, the floor of the money-
box turned gently round in her hand, and the great
secret was revealed. "Good," she cried, her face
lighting up, "now I shall be able to put some money
into it. This is a sensible sort of money-box."
"Yes," I said, "you were always lucky. Think of
all the other poor children slaving away with tin-
openers and screw-drivers. If parents only knew,
they would realize that the ordinary money-box is
a waste not only of their money but of their children's time." "Most grown-up people are silly,"
said my niece, as she pushed a penny through the slit
in the box and shook it so as to make it rattle.

Is this, then, the universal experience? Has no
child ever saved money in a money-box? The
money-box, I fancy, is not a natural inhabitant of
the nursery, but is a monument of worldly wisdom
set up there in the guise of a toy by crafty parents. I
doubt if any child, on being asked to choose a gift,

ever asked for a money-box. Not that children invariably dislike money-boxes when they get them. I
seem to remember enjoying the contemplation of a
new money-box and dreaming that it was already full
before I had dropped the first penny into it. Children have visions like their elders, and the vision of
riches begins to be attractive long before one has
ceased to eat liquorice alphabets. There is always
something that costs a little more than the pennies
of the day will run to—a toy revolver, a concertina,
a fishing-rod, a huge Roman candle, a watch, a new
sort of knife, a three-cornered Cape of Good Hope
stamp; and even a child soon learns that twelve pennies make a shilling, and that twenty shillings make
a pound, and that these vast sums can be achieved
by saving. A child, looking through the slit of a
money-box, can see a considerable extent of Paradise. On the other hand, there are Paradises less
out of reach in every confectioner's window and in
every advertisement of bargains in stamps at the
beginning of the *Boy's Own Paper*. It is difficult
even in later life to give up the positively delightful
present for the sake of the superlatively delightful
future. In childhood, one frail human being at least
found it impossible. Never once, I am confident,
was I able to buy anything out of savings. Never,
after the first few days of saving, did I look on a
money-box as anything but an enemy to be outwitted
and, if necessary, to be destroyed. As a rule, the
money-box was a small tin drum. When once the
pennies were in, you might hold the box upside down

and shake it for an hour without tempting a single coin to fall out. Then you got a knife and tried to tease one of the pennies gently to stand on its edge above the slit and to glide forth into the light of day. I am afraid I was a poor artificer, for even this usually failed with me. There are few things more exasperating than to have had a penny on the side of your knife time after time for a hundred times, and to see it always, just as it seemed about to behave like a Christian at last, disappear into the tenebrous fastnesses of the money-box. One of the sorrows of Tantalus must have been to possess a money-box full of pennies, and, when he felt a longing for coconut chips, always to be able to get a penny nearly, but not quite, out. I, for my part, could never endure this sort of thing for very long. The more the money-box defied me, the more determined I became, and, if I could not get at the pennies with a knife, I went over to the cupboard and took out the Young Craftsman's Box of Tools, and armed myself with a chisel. It is my firm conviction that no money-box was ever made that could stand out against a chisel. With a chisel you can either prise the top of the box off or, better still, you can widen the slit till the pennies drop out as easily as pigeons fly out of a pigeon-loft. The box, it is true, never looks the same again in either case. But to prise the lid off ruins it for ever, whereas the enlargement of the slit merely leaves it with a grotesque and irregular mouth. The untampered-with slit of a tin money-box with its prim, tight, cruel, ungenerous lips is reminiscent of Mr. Murdstone. With the help of a chisel it becomes transformed in the course of a few minutes into a mouth that can laugh—generous, Falstaffian, a partner in mischief. It also becomes immensely more useful to the child who owns it. Before, it was a mere nuisance, with all the vices and none of the virtues of an ornament. Now, it is a highly serviceable money-box—a money-box which you can either put pennies into or take pennies out of as you please.

It is a nice point in ethics whether it is dishonest to rob one's own money-box. Obviously, each of us consists of two selves—the self that wishes to save and the self that wishes to spend—and one of them differs as much from the other as a man does from his first cousin. Not only this, but each of them distrusts and is hostile to the other. The self that saves feels himself thwarted at every turn by the self that spends, and the self that spends is irritated by the knowledge that the self that saves is constantly watching him and grudging him every penny in his fingers. When the self that spends sees the self that saves stealthily slipping a penny into the money-box, he longs to cry: "Stop, thief! That belongs to me"; and when the self that saves sees the self that spends forcing pennies out of the money-box with a chisel, he, too, feels like crying out in his anguish: "Stop, thief! Everything in that box belongs to me." Theirs is, indeed, a tragic position, each of them serving a life-sentence in the other's hated company and as unable to escape from his neighbour as one of the Siamese twins. Luckily, at an early period in life, one of them usually gains predominance over the other, and bullies him into silence. Life would be intolerable if our two selves were for ever dragging each other into court and laying complaints against each other before that grave magistrate, conscience. I do not remember at what date the self that spends won a complete victory in my bosom over the self that saves, but I know that it was a Waterloo. I am as avaricious as anybody, and I love money more than can be expressed in prose; but I have no talent for saving it, and the only money I ever hoarded was money that I had had no time to spend within the narrow compass of a twenty-four hours' day. It was in vain that you would have told me, even at the age of ten, that "many a mickle makes a muckle," or that you would have given me an edifying book about a poor boy who became rich because he always remembered the proverb, "Take care of the pence, and the pounds will take care of themselves." I, too, desired to be rich, but I hoped it would happen by a miracle. It would have seemed to me a kind of meanness to deny my stomach a bar of chocolate or a box of sherbet merely in order that at some future date I might be prosperous and, perhaps, even a millionaire. It would have seemed like saving at the price of the sufferings of a friend. Why, after all, should the stomach suffer in the interests of the pocket? The stomach is human, sensitive and warm. The pocket is inhuman, unfeeling and cold. It is better that the pocket should serve the stomach than that the stomach should serve the pocket. Every child who has ever broken into its own money-box knows this.

And yet there must be some pleasure in saving money, for many people would rather do this than go to the theatre or travel or buy books or drink Burgundy. Probably the best people like doing it, because they are thinking of their children's future or want to help some cause that they have at heart. But there are also people who enjoy saving money for no other reason than the pleasure of saving money. It is a passion like drink, and a hobby like collecting old china. It is probably a fairly common passion, and a good many novelists from Balzac to Mr. Arnold Bennett have made it a dominant theme in fiction. Does it usually begin, I wonder, with a money-box? When Cruikshank became a fanatical teetotaller, he drew a series of horrifying pictures, showing the progress of the love of liquor from the cradle to the grave. The first scene, so far as I can remember, represented a child in arms being dosed with liquor by well-meaning but foolish parents. In that early sip was the forecast of the drunkard's doom. Can it be that the early gift of a money-box is as fatal a kindness? Imagine another Cruikshank drawing the Miser's Progress in a score of scenes, with the first scene showing a benevolent grandfather holding out a harmless-looking tin money-box to an infant scarce able to walk. Ten years later, the boy is putting a button into the collection-plate in order to save a penny.

In another ten years, he is smoking no cigarettes
except those he gets from his friends. By the age of
forty he has a substantial banking account, but he
persuades himself that he is so poor that he never
goes to the theatre, never rides in a taxi, and never
invites a friend to dinner. By sixty, he is a rich
man and is convinced that he is all but a pauper.
He gives up his morning paper and goes and reads
the papers in the Free Library for the sake of economy. By eighty, he is as great a wreck through
abstinence as it is possible to be through self-indul-
gence—a man who has always had plenty of money
and never knew how to spend it—a wastrel who
never wasted a penny—a monument of selfish self-
denial. It is a sad story, and should be a warning
to parents to think twice before placing so perilous
a gift as a money-box in the innocent hands of children. At least, if they do, the gift should always
be accompanied by a box of tools, containing a chisel,
a tin-opener, and a screwdriver. With these, a
money-box can do a child very little harm. The only
money-box consonant with virtue is a box out of
which one can get money when one wants it.

## The Life of Sensations

THERE is nothing that destroys the excitement
of motoring more surely than good roads and
careful driving. Luckily in France—at least, in the
part of France in which I have been studying the
rainfall during a typical twentieth-century summer—
good roads are few and careful drivers would be
warned by the police as obstructors of the traffic.
The main roads are, in a good many places, much
as they were when Julius Cæsar divided Gaul into
three parts. They do not merely contain ruts and
hollows as large as a baby's bath. They are also
full of deep pits—pits so deep that you dare scarcely
look over the edge for fear of feeling giddy. If you
did look into one of them, you would need a tele-
scope to see to the bottom, and probably you would
then descry the tiny figure of a man who, having
fallen in, had been vainly calling for help for days.
If you drive over this kind of road even at thirty
miles an hour, you enjoy all the ups and downs of
the roughest kind of Channel crossing. The very
swish of a wheel through one of the flooded pits
produces a wave that washes right over the rocking
car. As the French chauffeur plunges ahead, his
eyes are alight with a fierce excitement, and he keeps
calling to you through the roar and rattle
of the storm: *"C'est très dangereux, monsieur—*

*très dangereux."* You shout back, *"Oui,"* and hope
that, now that he has noticed it, he will slow down
a little. But he goes swiftly ahead, shouting things
about *"les grands trous"* and *"les bosses"* and, as
the car is swung sideways by one of them, excitedly
screams: *"Voilà,"* and puts on the accelerator. He
goes on repeating that these are *"très mauvaises
routes"* and shouting, *"très dangereux"* in a cres-
cendo till you begin to see the words in capital letters. You flash past a signpost warning you that a
crossing is coming. The sign looks horribly like
the crossbones in a letter threatening death. Again
you hope that he has noticed it, but you don't know
the French for "crossroads" and so cannot ask him.
He puts on speed in the evident determination not
to let any car coming in a sideways direction pass
the crossing before him. You rise a little in your
seat to try to see over the hedges that hide the side-
roads from your view. You prick your ears for the
sound of approaching wheels or the honk of a horn.
You try to make up your mind whether in the event
of a collision the car that is going faster is the one
that is likely to do the more damage or to suffer it.
To do it, you hope. You are now past the crossing
in safety, and you sink back in your seat in a luxury
of reaction. You begin to take an interest in the
needle of the speedometer which swings and sways
between 70 and 80. It certainly seems very fast,
and, as you turn the kilometres into miles in your
head, you realize that it is even faster than you
feared. You wish the chauffeur would not be quite

so reckless. Suppose a tyre should burst. As you fly past, an elderly peasant skips out of the way and falls back against a ditch, waving a stick and cursing. You agree with the elderly peasant. Just then, miles ahead of you along the sand-coloured road, you see a speck no bigger than a midge. The chauffeur sees it too, and puts on the accelerator. Gradually, it becomes about the size of a fly. The chauffeur becomes excited and puts on the accelerator again. You dash forward, at such a pace that you scarcely know whether you are passing dry land or sea, and the speck in the distance increases to the largeness of a man's head. You now know that it is another motor-car and that you are chasing it. You begin somehow to long to overtake it. The motor-car ahead of you must be going at about sixty miles an hour. You wonder whether your own man couldn't do seventy. Joy, you are catching up. The car takes a flying leap into the air, and you do not know for the moment whether it will fall on its feet or its side or upside down. *"Un grand trou,"* shouts the chauffeur when you have reached the earth again. *"Très dangereux,"* you shout back with enthusiasm, holding on your hat. *"Très dangereux,"* he replies in the same spirit, accelerating the accelerator. *"Chassez,"* you shout to him encouragingly. *"Oui, monsieur,"* he replies, kicking something to see if he can make the car go faster. Happily, he can, and the other car becomes larger and larger as the road becomes hilly, and you pursue it, making a noise like a fleet of battleplanes shaving the roofs

of a town. It disappears round a curve and over
the crest of a hill. You follow, and perceive it
flying down the hill at a pace that has never yet been
achieved outside the pages of fiction. You give
chase, the four wheels off the ground, reaching the
bottom of the hill in a whirl of resolve either to
overtake the enemy or to perish in the attempt, and
in another kilometre you are on its heels, the stones
flying against your mudguards and the speedometer
rocking backwards and forwards as though it were
recording the beatings of an exhausted heart. Neck
and neck, you pass a crossroad together with its
sign of dead men's bones. And, after that, with
another access of speed, you honk your horn vic-
toriously, and sweep past, like a Rolls-Royce over-
taking a taxicab. Your car seems just to kiss the
mudguard of the other as it flies past. "*Très dangereux,*" you call out breathlessly. "*Très dangereux,*" the chauffeur agrees with a happy smile. "*Très
mauvaises routes,*" you say to him ecstatically. "*Oui,
oui, très mauvaises routes,*" he replies, and puts on
the accelerator. "*Des grands trous,*" you shout.
"*Voilà,*" he cries, as the car, having just escaped
from one, rears and bucks.

But, alas, it is impossible in English prose to convey the excitement of motoring in France. It is at
once extraordinarily terrifying and extraordinarily
pleasant. You keep thinking "If I live through this,
it will be great fun." But you never feel quite certain that you will live through it. And, when you
come to one of those steep, narrow, corkscrew roads,

that go downhill for miles and miles—roads that
are marked with a "Z" on the signposts—you are
prepared for the worst at every turn of the road.
You also wish that the chauffeur did not think it
necessary to take both hands off the wheel and ges-
ticulate every time he speaks. You say to him,
*"Beaucoup de tournes—très brusques."* Immediately, he is waving both hands in the air to express
his opinion of the turns, and only takes the wheel
again in time to twist round the next bend. *"Très
dangereux,"* you cry to him, when your heart has
recovered from its dropped beat. He again takes
both hands from the wheel, waves them above his
head, repeating, *"Très—très dangereux!"* and seizes
the wheel just in time to duck under the bow of a
suddenly-appearing char-à-banc. In the end you decide that it is safer not to address him at all, and
you do not until he goes bumping over a railway
crossing after a sharp turn, while three women in
black fly screaming from under the wheels. The
chauffeur is indignant, and calls out: *"Je ne l'ai pas
vu."* You call back, *"Très dangereux."* *"Très dangereux,"* he yells frantically, and speeds on towards
the next crossroads. Luckily, there are comparatively few people who use motor-cars in France, and
most of the crossroads are bare of hedges, so that
one has a good chance of seeing an approaching
vehicle before the collision has occurred. Still, so
far as I could see, every motorist takes it for granted
that the other motorists will take all the steps necessary to avoid the collision. Our chauffeur certainly

drove as though there were not another vehicle on the roads of France, and, if we had not an accident, it was only because there was nothing to run into at the really dangerous places. The worst of it was that the chauffeur kept giving me statistics of the various accidents that had taken place at various *"dangereux"* corners and that my French is so bad that I could not be sure whether five people were killed at such and such a spot every day, or only every year. I shall really have to learn French before I risk another motor-ride along the French roads. Disciples of M. Coué will realize how unnerving it is to carry on a prolonged conversation, consisting of little more than a repetition of the words, *"Très dangereux."*

But how safe it felt to be back at dinner in the hotel! How delicious the soup tasted! How mellow the *vin ordinaire!* After dinner, somebody proposed to tell fortunes by cards, but I firmly refused to be led back out of my sense of sweet security into a life of sensations with aces of spades and dark women casting a cloud over the future. "Then what about *planchette*?" I was asked. I shrink from dealings with spirits, but I hate being a spoilsport, so consented, and in a few minutes an alphabet had been placed in a ring round the table and we were all pressing a finger lightly on an inverted wine glass in the centre. The glass began to stir uneasily, and, on being spoken to and asked who it was, it slowly spelt out the name, "Clemence Dane." It said that it wanted to talk about books,

and, on being asked what it thought of Mr. Forster's
*Passage to India,* replied: "Good, but have not
read it." It then became frivolous, and, to every
question that was addressed to it, replied with the
one word, "Cabbage." If you asked its opinion of
anybody, it immediately spelt out either "Cabbage"
or "A bad cabbage," as though it were determined
on mocking us. As all present had given their words
of honour not to push or pull the glass, it may be
assumed that none of them were deliberately trifling,
but the nonsense became so monotonous in the end
that we bade the spirit farewell and called up another in its stead. We asked the new spirit who it
was, and it replied: "A fay." We asked it what it
wished to talk to us about, and to our horror the
glass immediately spelt out the words, "A bad cabbage." One lady went pale and said: "This may be
a warning." Another declared that cabbage was a
vegetable never served at the hotel, and that the
whole thing was absurd. We pursued our investiga-
tions, however, and were told that the cabbage was to
appear during dinner on the following evening, and
that none of us must on any account touch it. Being
of a humane disposition, we asked: "But what about
the other people in the hotel? Won't they be in danger too?" The glass spelt "Yes." "And, if a cabbage
appears, must we tell them not to eat it?" The glass
spelt: "You must warn." "But surely," we protested, "Madame P."—the hotel-keeper's wife—
"will be very much annoyed with us." The glass
replied: "You must vex." It is all very well to mock

at human credulity, but I am convinced that every one of us was apprehensive during all that night and all the next day lest a cabbage should appear at the evening meal, and one of us should have to rise and denounce it in public. I certainly was feeling ill at ease during the first two courses of the dinner, though I knew very well that, if a cabbage did appear, the task of denouncing it would be deputed to a woman. Then, as the vegetables were being brought in, a girl who had a good view of the door suddenly cried: "Look, it *is* cabbage after all." Everyone at the table started and stared at everybody else with a wild surmise, till someone had the courage to look round and in a moment uttered a cry of joy: "No, it's only runner beans." Once again, as during the motor-ride, we enjoyed the blessed relief of those who have escaped disaster by the skin of their teeth. We called for *vieille cure,* and another one, that evening with a good conscience. And after that we went to another room and had a long and interesting conversation with the spirit of Alcibiades.

## The Ghost

IT is, I fancy, a common enough experience, after avoiding a man during his lifetime, to feel a sharp pang of regret on hearing that he is dead. While he was alive, ten minutes in his company were an eternity: now that he himself has become a piece of eternity, how pitifully brief his whole life seems in retrospect! A dead bore is no longer a bore: in dying he has done one of the three most interesting things that it is possible for a man to do. We meet other men who avoided him in life, and it is of the dead bore that we all find ourselves talking. We do not, it is true, attempt to defend him or to make out that we ever found his company exhilarating. But our very accusations have a note of guilt in them. We say aloud to each other: "He was really terrible. Ten minutes in his company made you feel you were going mad." But all the time we are thinking to ourselves: "Poor chap! Why on earth didn't I see him the last time he called? If I had known he was going to die so soon, I should certainly have seen him. After all, what are ten minutes in a lifetime?" We begin to feel a little tenderly towards him—to remember him as a rather forlorn and friendless figure. We recall the pathetic pleasure he got from boring people—how he never noticed the drawn and haggard faces of those who were listening or doing their best to listen to him, their grimaces of agony that were meant for smiles, the appeal for mercy in their melancholy eyes. He was always sufficiently interested for the whole company, and he laughed enough for everybody present. He was invariably the happiest person in the room—often the only happy person. He did not, apparently, notice that he had no friends; he took it for granted that all of us to whom he talked were his friends. Except just towards the end. He seemed then to have had an inkling of the truth—to have noticed that it was more difficult to find a listener than it used to be and that he was oftener solitary. He had lost the self-confidence of the true bore, and had the beginnings of the air of a broken man. "I wish to Heaven I had seen him that last time he called." Vain regrets! He is now in better company than he ever made miserable on earth. He is with Helen of Troy and Alexander of Macedon and Dr. Johnson. Perhaps, he is boring them. But no; that would mean that they were in Hell.

I heard lately of the death of a man who was famous in the circle of his acquaintances, not as a bore, but as a borrower. I doubt if he had any other existence except as a borrower. No one who has mentioned him to me for many years has told me a single fact about him except that he borrowed money from them. No breath of scandal touched him. If he had any sins, they were unknown except to himself. If he had any virtues, they were unknown except to himself. Nothing seems ever to have hap-

pened to him except that he borrowed money. I am
not sure that he even needed the money he borrowed.
If he met you in the street and stopped you, I am
fairly sure that, when he asked you for a loan, it was
often out of inveterate habit and because he did not
know what else to talk about. Or it may have been a
game of skill that he played. He saw an acquain-
tance approaching and said to himself: "Hullo,
here's old——. Good joke if I could touch him for a
quid." And then began a battle of wits as enjoyable
to him as a game of chess to better men, and, if he
went away with as much as half-a-crown in his
pocket, he felt that he had won.

When I knew him first, he was working in the
same London office with me, and earning a living
by drawing horrible pictures of villains threatening
honest women and the usual kind of illustrations for
serial stories in cheap papers. That was near the
beginning of the century. Neither I nor anybody
else in the office knew him very well, for, though he
was always merry and bright, he lived a life of his
own outside office hours. Sometimes he would come
into the office in the morning and say: "Had too
much beer last night, old man." But he never drank
beer with us. "In buckets, my lad, in buckets," he
would confide. "D'you know what's the best thing
to do after you've had a dozen of Bass?" And he
would produce a little glass jar of liver-pills and tap
it affectionately. "Take four or five of these before
you get into bed, and you'll wake up in the morning
as fresh as paint—as fresh as paint, my boy." No

one, however, had ever seen him under the influence
of alcohol, and most of us believed that his tales of
drinking were mere boasting. Ultimately an accident occurred to the paper and I lost sight of him,
and he remained in my memory only as a myth about
a dozen of Bass, for he had not at that time begun
to play the game of borrowing money. Then, one
evening, many years later, when I was jumping on to
a bus in the Strand, I felt a hand on my sleeve, and
looking round, saw the smiling face that had so often
sung the praises of liver-pills. "You don't remember
me, old man?" he said. "Of course, you don't! You
do? Eh, lad, we've had some times together. Have
you a minute to spare? Come over here and tell me
about yourself. I've often said to myself: 'I wonder
what's happened to old Y. I wonder if he ever remembers his old pal, Jack Straw?' Let's have a
good look at you, old man. How long is it since
I saw you last? Twenty years, and you don't look a
day older. Eh, lad"—holding me by the arms and
looking at me admiringly—"this is good. But, tell
me, how are things? Doing pretty well?" "Oh, not
so bad," I told him, "—scraping along more or less.
But tell me about yourself. What have *you* been
doing all this time?" He drew me up against a shop
front, then closed one eye and lowered his voice
mysteriously. "To tell you the truth, old man," he
said, as if imparting a secret not to be shared with
the passers-by, "I've been through it. I've been
through 'ell. But it's all right now";—and he
winked hard at me again—"I've just had a commis-

sion that'll keep me going for the next three months. But you know what it is. The money's there all right, and I could get as much as I need by asking for it. But I don't want them to think, 'Old Straw's hard up. Let's cut down his prices.' So, if you happen to have a loose dollar about you, old man, and if you give me your address, I'll come round and let you have it back by Tuesday."

He undoubtedly kept his word about calling round. When his little straight-backed figure was shown into the room, I was agreeably surprised, for it is not often that people who have borrowed money keep their word about paying it back. "Eh, lad," he said, gazing round with soft-eyed admiration, "this looks prosperous. I like to see an old pal getting on. But," he said, sitting down and drawing his chair nearer to mine, "what I wanted to see you about was this, and I don't want you to let it go any further." I promised secrecy. "Well, old man, I thought to myself, 'Old Y. won't mind if I speak to him quite frankly. He'll remember the days when we were pals together.'" I began to fear the worst. He hitched his chair still nearer, dropped a solemn and confidential wink, and lowered his voice almost to a whisper. "Fact is, old man, I've the deuce of a lot of money owing to me. A matter of a hundred or a hundred and fifty quid. But you know how it is, old man. It's not policy to ask for it. Looking hard up doesn't pay. And what I was wondering was, old man, whether you could let me have fifty quid till next Monday. Between you and me, I'm in a bit of a fix. I know, old man, you're the sort of chap who would do anything to help a pal and I tell you quite frankly that, if you can let me have the fifty quid till Monday, you'll be doing me a service, and I shan't forget it. There's nothing like straight talk between pals, is there, old man?" And he fixed his eyes on mine with a smile partly of anxiety and partly of the deepest affection. I could not help laughing, for all the wealth I possessed in the world was a small overdraft at the bank. I told him how things stood. I also lied to him because of the disturbed look in his eyes. "If I had fifty pounds," I said, "or fifty shillings, I'd be delighted to lend it to you." He recovered himself and nodded his head sympathetically. "I know you would, old man," he said. "I didn't realize you were so hard up. And do you know what I'm going to do, laddie?" He leaned forward, laid his hand on my knee and shut one eye. "As soon as I draw my hundred and fifty quid, do you know the first thing I'm going to do with it? I'm going to come round to this office, and you shall have fifty of it." "Oh, no, no," I protested in embarrassment. "Oh, but you shall," he declared firmly, slapping me on the knee: "What the 'ell's the good of pals if they don't help each other when they can? But look here, old man"—dropping his voice again—"now that that's all arranged—you don't happen to have a spare quid about you?" "I'm absolutely broke," I assured him. "I say, old man," he protested, "I wish I had a few quid I could let you have. If ever you're hard up, sonny, come to Jack

Straw, and, if he has a quid in the world, you shall
have it. You shall, old man. For the sake of the
old times. Next Monday, old man, you shall have
that fifty. I wouldn't call you a pal if you refused
it." The voice dropped again. "Do you think you
could manage half a quid, old man?" We parted on
affectionate terms, he loudly extolling the good old
days, when we had had such times together. After
that, we met frequently, though not more often than
I could help. His conversation was all "old man,"
"pals," "eh, lads," "the old times," leading inevitably
up to the request for a sum that varied from half-a-
crown to a pound. He always had the same story—
that the tide had at last turned, that he was making
pots of money, but that it was bad policy for an
artist to press people for payment. And he never
took the smallest sum without saying: "Some day
I'll do as much for you, old man." One day he
called round with a parcel under his arm, and said,
"Look here, old man, you're fond of pictures, aren't
you?" He opened the parcel, saying, "Something
to show you, laddie," took out a water-colour and
stood it up against the back of a chair. It was a
picture of a pond and water-lilies such as a pavement
artist might have painted. He looked from the
picture to me with the lovelight in his eyes. "Isn't
it bonny?" he asked, cocking his head sideways at it.
I said it was a beauty. "How much would you say
that little thing's worth, old man?" he asked me.
"I don't know much about the price of pictures," I
told him. "Five quid, would you say?" he pressed

me. "Yes, I should think so," I said for the sake of
peace. "You shall have it for two-ten," he declared
nobly. "But I've no room in the house for any more
pictures," I protested. "That's all right," he replied
with a heavy wink; "you can sell it and make a bit."
I met him in the street a few days later. He came
up to me with friendship written all over his face.
"Look here, old man," he said, "you've been a good
pal to me." "Oh, no, no," I repeated, the customary
formula. "But you have, old man, and, if you forget
it, I don't. Now, look here, I would like to do some
little thing for you in return. You remember that
picture of mine that you said was worth a fiver?"
"Yes," I said, hesitatingly. "You shall have it for
a quid," said he, laying his hand on my shoulder. I
assured him that I hadn't a pound to bless myself
with. He looked grave for a moment. "I tell you
what I'm going to do, old man," he said, after a
pause. "I saw you fancied that little picture, and
I'm going to make you a present of it. One good
turn deserves another."

He had a curious talent for making you feel his
debtor—offering you large hypothetical loans and
loading you with ungiven gifts. But, in the end, like
his other acquaintances, I hardened myself against
his appeals. When I met him in the street and refused him, however, he laughed and winked at me
as if he had only been teasing me, and renewed the
request in the best of spirits a few days later. I
refused him with all the better conscience because I
was convinced that he was earning a living and only

borrowed money because he had a kind of habit of borrowing, and preferred spending other people's money to spending his own. And now I am not sure. Was he really hard up? Did he need that last half-sovereign as badly as he declared? I cannot help regretting that final coldness. I am repentant before his ghost. May he have better luck in his acquaintances among the shades!

## The New Cat

CATS are the enemies of conversation. I have a friend who, after an absence of many years, has lately settled down in London, with a wife, a cat and a garden. Owing to the cat, I doubt if our friendship can continue. I called to see him and was shown into the garden, where he and his wife were sitting in deck chairs. How many things there were that I wished to talk to him about! How happily I looked forward to hearing the names of old friends and old places on his lips and to telling him all the news of the deaths and divorces that had taken place since he had been lost to civilization in Buenos Aires! I even looked forward to meeting his wife, though I do not on the whole like my friends to marry. We had hardly shaken hands and sat down, however, than he glanced at his wife with a look of alarm and said, "Where's Oliver Cromwell?" His wife looked round the garden apprehensively and began calling "Olly! Olly! Olly!" and, when there was no answer, said: "Where can he have gone?" Then followed an exciting dialogue of this kind. "He can't have got through the fence into the next garden." "I saw him only a minute ago." "Perhaps, he's in the ash. He was up there when I came out this morning, and I had to fetch the ladder to bring him down." "Olly, Olly, Olly!" (in a woman's voice). "Oliver Crom-

well! Oliver Cromwell!" (in a man's shout). "Oh,
there he is, coming out of the lupin!" "Naughty
Oliver Cromwell, where have you been?" "Puss,
puss, puss, puss, puss!" "Where's the ball, Stella?
Here you are, Oliver, here's something to play with.
You mustn't interrupt the conversation, you know,"
and he rolled the ball gently over the grass. The
kitten watched it, fascinated. It flattened itself on
the grass, stretched out its neck, cocked its ears,
stared with wide eyes, and moved its tail in
cruel anticipation. Then it dashed towards the ball,
and, just as it reached it, made a sideways spring with
arched back and avoided it, and sat down and began
to lick its right foreleg from the knee downwards, as
though it had forgotten all about the ball. "Well,"
said my friend with self-satisfaction, "what do you
think of Oliver Cromwell? Isn't he a beauty?" I
agreed that he was. "Look, look," his wife interrupted us, and, as the kitten began to flatten himself into position for another rush at the ball, she
gurgled as if to herself: "Oh, he was *such* a darling!
He was *such* a darling!" This time the kitten did
leap on to the ball, caught it in its front paws, lifted
it in the air, turned a back somersault with it, rolled
on the grass, and then, as if in terror, fled for all it
was worth into the Solomon's seal in the flower
border and, hidden among the stalks, looked out on
its late prey, like a tiger concealing itself in the
jungle. These evolutions were received by my friend
and my friend's wife with shouts of laughter. My
friend said that they ought really to have called the

kitten Cinquevalli. The way it juggled with the ball, he declared, was simply wonderful. "It was *such* a clever little cat," his wife began to talk to herself again; "much cleverer than Cinquevalli. Oh, *much* cleverer," she declared, reaching out her hand and taking the kitten into her lap. As she stroked it, it padded up and down with its paws on her dress, arched its back at every stroke of her hand, and purred. My friend watched it in a state of fatuous and happy idolatry. I half-expected him and his wife to begin purring at any moment, too. It was obvious that the purring of the kitten had a hypnotic effect on them, and I doubt if either of them remembered that I was present.

A housemaid came out with the tea-things, and she, too, when she had put the tray down looked at the kitten with fatuous and idolatrous eyes. It seemed to be with difficulty that she tore herself away eventually, and, even when she reached the house, she looked back as if she could scarcely bear to leave the wonderful presence. "You remember Jack Robinson's cats?" I said to my friend as a way of getting back to normal conversation, so that I could ask him whether he had heard of poor Jack's death in a yachting accident. "I hope," said his wife, "that you're not going to pretend that anybody ever had such a perfectly wonderful cat as Oliver Cromwell. Because," she added, rubbing the kitten under the chin, "we simply won't believe it. Isn't that so, Oliver?" "Poor old Jack—" I began again. "I never understood his passion for cats," said my friend, "—at least, not till we got this little beast." "You mustn't call Oliver Cromwell a little beast," protested his wife. "You heard about Jack's death?" I said. "Jack dead! No. How? Look out!" he roared, as the kitten sprang from his wife's lap and made after a bee across the grass. "I always thought kittens had more sense than to chase bees. He'll get stung some day. Poor old Jack!" as the bee—and the kitten—escaped; "this is the first I heard of it." I told him how the accident had taken place—how Jack had been knocked overboard, apparently stunned, for he had sunk like a stone. His wife, I presume, was not listening, for, as at the end of my story he and I were sunk in a momentary silence, she broke in with: "I declare he's caught a bee this time. Poor little pet! Poor, silly little pet!" she cried, hurrying over and fondling the kitten where it was feeling its lower lip with its ankle as if it had been stung. My friend went over and joined her and said, "Let's see if we can see the sting. Perhaps we can pull it out." But just then the kitten saw a cabbage-white butterfly and dashed off out of their hands in pursuit. They laughed delightedly. "I don't believe he was stung at all," said my friend. "Poor old Jack! It's hard to imagine him dead. You remember the day he and Bobbie Stone swam out to the Skerries? What happened to Bobbie?" "He was murdered," I told him, "during a row in India." "Good God!" said my friend. "Olly! Olly! Olly!" called his wife excitedly. "Oh, do go and catch him, Tom, or he'll be into the next garden."

Tom rose and bolted across the grass, and was just
in time to seize Oliver Cromwell as he had got his
head through a hole in the fence.  He brought him
back and put him into his wife's lap.  "Poor old
Bobbie!" he said, obviously moved.  "It's extraordinary that no one ever wrote to tell me.  I often
wondered what had become of him.  He seemed such
a splendid chap at school."  His wife, too, was
evidently awed as even strangers are on hearing of a
tragedy.  "Was he a great friend of yours, Tom?"
she asked gently.  "He was, at school," said Tom.
"After that we didn't see much of each other."  "He
was the best all-round scholar and athlete of his
year," I told her.  "What a terrible thing to happen
to him," she said, stroking the kitten.  It saw a fly
buzzing round her head, climbed up her shoulder in
pursuit, and walked round the back of her neck.
"Do rescue me, Tom," she cried.  "He's got his
claws in my neck."  Tom seized the kitten by the
scruff of the neck, held it up and looked at it re-
proachfully, and said: "Now look here, old chap, go
and play with your ball and leave us in peace for a
few minutes.  I told you you mustn't interrupt the
conversation."

But what cat ever cared what anybody told it?
I did succeed in the course of the afternoon in telling
Tom how one friend had become a County Court
judge, and another a doctor, and how another was
making a fortune as a journalist in America.  But I
did it to a constant accompaniment of "Pussy, pussy,
pussy!" "Olly, Olly, Olly!" "He's rolling on the

nemophila. Go and take him off, Tom," "I do love
a cat when its tail stands up like a note of inter-
rogation," "Naughty Oliver Cromwell! you mustn't
try to catch sparrows," that made me feel as exhausted as if I had been shouting for hours to a deaf
man in a gale. "Come again soon," said my friend's
wife, as we shook hands, "Mind, we expect you
every Sunday," said Tom heartily. "Come back,
Oliver Cromwell," his wife's voice reached us as we
disappeared. "Take care that he doesn't get out
of the front door, Tom."

I am myself an admirer of cats, but I do not like
them as part of a conversation. I do not think that
cats should be spoken to in the presence of visitors.
They should be seen and not talked about. Whether
I shall be able to live up to these principles, however,
now that a perfectly wonderful kitten has come to
live in my house, I do not know. It is so charming,
so fearless, so restless, so playful. There were
already two small black cats in the house. One of
them was a stray, given to us by the butcher. Its ears
are three times the ordinary size, and it has a tail like
a rat, so that one does not draw the attention of
visitors to it, but it is so gentle, so free from malice—
except against birds and insects—that one cannot
help liking it. The other, Mrs. Blacktoes, is very
beautiful and very cross. She came into the house
one night when we were calling Felix, and she has
stayed ever since. But she never purrs except at
meal-times, and she growls and runs away if you
attempt to stroke her. She must have come from a

home, I imagine, where no one ever touched her except to pull her tail.  But as for the new kitten, Tiger, with his striped body and his white dickie, he is so light as he feels his way about the new world, testing every inch as he advances with his feather-weight of a paw, that he seems no more substantial than a thistledown.  It is impossible to look at a book while he is in the room.  What chair does he not investigate?  How inquisitively he examines the bookshelves, cautiously pressing himself into every vacant space!  How he dances after the moths on his hind legs in the evening!  How happily he plays by the hour with the ball of paper that swings like a pendulum on a string from the arm of a chair!  He examines the string and fights it and bites it.  He jumps on to the chair and studies the knot by which it is tied.  He lies on his back on the floor and kicks the ball of paper.  He sits down and taps it like a tennis-ball with his paw as it passes.  He goes to a distance and pounces on it.  He seizes it and rolls about like a footballer.  I think I shall invite Tom and his wife to come and see me, while Tiger is still a novelty.  It would be a punishment, and, until I have punished them, I doubt if I shall be able to forgive them.

## The Idea

IF you go to the south of France in January, you will be less than human if you are not charmed by the spectacle of the orange-trees with their brilliant ripe fruits hanging like toys among the little green leaves. The orange-tree seems to concentrate in itself every delightful thing that we mean by the south. It is not only a tree but an image. It is as though each individual fruit hanging in its branches were a small shining sun. If you were writing home, you would only need to say that there was an orange-tree heavy with fruit in the garden below your bedroom window in order to conjure up a picture of seas and rivers flowing into them, extravagantly blue, of a world that glowed with flowers, of indolence in daylong sunshine, of birds singing the songs of April and May while it is still winter. As for eating an orange freshly plucked from the tree, how desirable it seems! How pleasant to see the little mandarin nestling among its leaves on the fruit-dish! It is as attractive as a fruit out of a legend. You feel that it would be worth travelling hundreds of miles merely to eat such a fruit in such a setting.

And yet, after eating many oranges in such circumstances for the first time in my life, I must confess with regret that an orange fresh from the tree is not half so wonderful as the idea of an orange

fresh from the tree. There are few things in the
world more disappointing than these mandarins, or
tangerines—for I think a mandarin is only an inferior tangerine—that mean so much to the imagination and so little to the palate. You could buy far
better oranges in a London shop. One good Jaffa
orange is worth a dozen mandarins. Yet, somehow,
the act of eating a Jaffa orange in London does not
excite the fancy. A large orange, eaten in town, may
satisfy the palate, but it leaves the imagination cold.
So delightful is the idea of eating an orange fresh
from the tree, however, that not even after a score
of disappointments has one the heart to refuse the
small crumpled fruit that is served at the end of
every meal. Tangerines, it must also be admitted,
make an irresistible appeal to the imagination even
when one is not in an orange-growing country. Most
of us, I am sure, have loved them from childhood.
Perhaps, it is because they themselves are so tiny that
they seem properties of the world of childhood.
When we are children, we love everything that is
small as we ourselves are small. We love Shetland
ponies more than thoroughbreds, ducklings more
than geese, kittens more than elephants. The larger
things, much as we like them, are of a piece with the
lives of serious and grown-up people. The little
things are natural playthings, and we feel at play
when we look at them or touch them. That, I think,
rather than their exceptional fragrance, or the sweet-
ness of their juices, is the explanation of our love of
tangerines. Their size is so charming, indeed, that,

while we remain children, we resolutely refuse to admit that we have been disappointed just a little in eating them. At that age we can still eat with our imaginations, and our palates do not argue with and contradict us. If an orange is small and is wrapped in silver paper, that is enough for us. Given so much, we can pretend the rest. For us it is the diet of Paradise so long as it looks as if it were the diet of Paradise. I do not, I may say, wish to decry the tangerine as a fruit not worth eating. The flavour is agreeable enough, though not so agreeable as the smell. But, with all its virtues, the tangerine remains one of the inferior oranges, with an excess of seeds and a deficiency of liquor. I am sure there are many people who will contradict me on this point. All children will, and nearly all men and women who have preserved the happy childish gift of enjoying things without judging them—relying on memory and imagination rather than on the palate and supplying all the shortcomings of reality with good-natured makebelieve. Heaven forbid that I should destroy their illusions even about tangerines! But we who have been disillusioned must communicate our disillusion to each other. We do not boast: we merely confess. It is to our sorrow that we know with Plato that the perfect orange—the orange of the idea—hangs not on any tree in any earthly garden but exists only in Heaven.

Nor is the orange the only food of man that is more beautiful in the idea than in reality. The enjoyment of many of the things we eat and drink lies in the anticipation. How seldom does a cup of coffee equal the idea of a cup of coffee! Who does not love coffee as an idea? Who is not continually disappointed by coffee as a fact? If most of us go on drinking coffee, it is because we live in the perpetual pursuit of an idea, not because we have much hope that the next cup of coffee is going to be a good one. We know from experience that there is as much difference between the coffee we drink in restaurants and the coffee we drink in our imaginations as there is between war-time beer and nectar. But such idealists are mortals that we go on drinking it in restaurants, on railway trains, and even in lodgings. We should lose heart, perhaps, and take to milder liquors if it were not that every now and then we do get a cup of coffee in which the idea of coffee seems almost to have been realized on earth. How proud our host is as he explains how perfection was achieved! He talks as a teacher, like the wise men of old. At such a moment, surrounded by listening guests, he would not change places with Socrates. I doubt, however, if even he can make the perfect coffee except occasionally and by a happy accident. He remains a man puffed-up for the rest of his days, but, when we visit him again, the secret has vanished, and, though his guests praise him with lies, they pity him as a man who is living among illusions. If statistics could be compiled on the subject, I am sure it would be found that not more than one cup of coffee in a thousand that are made deserves to be called even tolerable. The rest are but a warm infusion with which we still our cravings. Sometimes, they smell like perfect coffee, and, if coffee were a perfume and not a drink, we should be happy. But, for the most part, they are of such a kind as, if a doctor were present and ordered us to harden our arteries with the poison no more, would make it easy for us to resolve to obey him.

Luckily for themselves, most human beings do not trust their palates on such matters, but easily find in food or drink the excellence they expect to find. If they are told that the coffee at such and such a restaurant is always good, it will always be good to them. They are the happy victims of suggestion. If they go to France, expecting the cheaper wines to be wonderful, they will praise enthusiastically wines such as you could get cheaply enough in the worst London wine-shops. Our pleasure in wine is largely pleasure in an idea. Few of us have a skilled palate in wine; I, for one, have not. I divide wines into two broad categories: wines that are drinkable and wines that aren't, like the Australian burgundy that I bought the other day. But I have heard men saying "Jolly good wine" as they drank a liquor that it would have been shameful to use as a rat-poison— nay, as a weed-killer. These are the idealists of the table in the ordinary sense of the word "idealists." They are the people who can mistake the most loathsome reality for the heavenly perfection of an idea. We all share their happiness to some extent, for we are all to some extent slaves of suggestion. I am in the unfortunate position, however, of being one of those people to whom it is easier to suggest that a thing is bad than that a thing is good. You could not make me enjoy eating a stale egg merely by saying "What a beautifully fresh egg!" But you could stop me from eating a fresh egg by saying, "That egg smells as if it were stale." Imagination can taint food for me more easily than it can sweeten it. The idea of a bad egg is so disgusting that it would outweigh the reality of the egg's freshness. But I do not find the idea of a fresh egg so intoxicating that it can make me forget that the egg is really stale.

Among foods that belong to the realm of ideas rather than of realities, I think, must be counted cakes of all sorts. I can see no other reason why one who loved cakes so greedily as I once loved them now cares so little for them. I still like the idea of a cake. I like to look into a confectioner's window. I like to go into a teashop, and, when I do, I have the ancient childish belief that the cakes on the other tables are beautiful. I am enough of an idealist to believe in the excellence of almost any cake that is out of reach. But no sooner is a cake on my own plate than I know it to be a deceiver. This is not the fair idea for which I hungered. This is a base compost of flour and sugar that may be a remedy against starvation, but that does not feed the mind. Some men gild their past with the belief that cakes are not so good as they used to be, but it seems to me more likely that cakes have remained the same, but that it is we who have changed. As children we ate, not cakes, but ideas; now we eat, not ideas, but cakes. We sought perfection and found only commonness. It is the old story. Gods and men, we are all deluded thus. Go over all the things you think you would like to eat and drink, and you will find that, in most cases, what you would like to eat or drink is not the thing in itself but the idea of the thing. There are few things but oysters and Peneau's sardines that survive the test of experience. Even salmon, I fancy, dwells in an ambiguous borderland among the things that are almost realities, but the beauty of which is too often only the enticing beauty of the idea. The conclusion of the matter is that, if one is really fond of food, it is better to read a cookery book than to go out to dinner. In the cookery book the most high-minded idealist will never be disappointed.

## The Professor

WHEN I read the obituary references to Sir
Samuel Dill, how vividly his figure came before me, pacing the streets of a modern city as
though he were a survivor from some older and more
gracious civilization! He might have been happy in
Athens; he might have been happy even in Oxford;
but in Belfast he had the air of a banished man.
If he talked to you about yourself, he had but one
message—"Escape. Fly while there is time." He
spoke again and again of "this *borné* atmosphere"
in such a fashion that I should have been exasperated
into a defence of my native city to any less imperious
man, for at the time I was more under the influence
of Mr. Kipling than of the authors in my Greek
course, and I believed that a walk down North Street
on Saturday night was quite as interesting as most of
the things that used to happen under the shadow of
the Parthenon. But there was nothing priggish or
lily-handed about Dill's passion for culture. Almost
he persuaded you to believe in culture as he surveyed
you with melancholy eyes and wistfully murmured
the name of Oxford as the city towards which you
should bend your steps, burden on back, in search of
salvation. He never became quite used to a world
in which a fair proportion of the men and youths
were not scholars and philosophers, or the satellites

of scholars and philosophers. Oxford first, then London, with a post in the Civil Service that would leave you plenty of leisure to read Greek and (if you could) to write English—such was the dream that he held before you to tempt you to spend your evenings over Herodotus instead of in the gallery of the Theatre Royal. Well, I have always been in love with Oxford, and, if posts in the Civil Service were given away for nothing, I should undoubtedly have filled one long ago. But these things, I knew, were not to be had save at the price of great labour, if they were to be had with that. Even so I became sufficiently infected with Dill's enthusiasm to see myself often in a day-dream settled in Oxford, having won a rich scholarship without doing any work whatever, and passing on from that into a highly-paid position in the Civil Service which, by a curious coincidence, also came to me without my needing to do any work for it. Few undergraduates have had so brilliant and, at the same time, so easy a career as I had at Oxford, and few Civil servants have had so comfortable a time in arm-chairs so stuffed with rose-leaves. Some day, perhaps, I shall write my reminiscences of Oxford and the Civil Service. They are all part of a dream that I had before I was twenty.

Not that Dill ever meant to encourage such visions of indolence. His view of life was a stern one. He kept his very class-room cold, with open windows that often let in an almost too bracing winter. There was no other room in Queen's in which the students

sat in such orderly awe and in which the student who
had come unprepared so wished to Heaven that he
had not come at all.  Dill spoke sometimes in sorrow,
and sometimes in anger, but always he treated any
sign of slackness as though it were a violation of
sacred things.  He regarded it as a crime even to
come unprepared on the first day after the Christmas
holidays.  I was once unfortunate enough to be asked
on such an occasion to read a passage from Thucyd-
ides that I was then seeing for the first time, and I
still remember the mournful gaze he turned on me
while he said in accents as if of passionate sorrow:
"Unstable as water, thou shalt not excel."  He was
especially impatient of students who came to his class
merely in order to acquire the minimum of Greek
that was necessary for a pass degree.  There were
a number of theological students who regarded a
knowledge of Greek merely as a necessary step on
the way up to a pulpit.  Many of the best scholars
were theological students, but there were other
ministers in the bud who cared neither for Homer
nor for Plato, except for the marks that were to be
got out of them.  To Dill these were the children of
outer darkness.  He loathed examinations, and he
could scarcely endure human beings who read Homer
not for poetry, but for marks.  "Why do you come
here?" he one day demanded of a young theologian
who showed himself unresponsive to the charms of
Greek culture.  "Do you come here expecting me to
cram you for a miserable examination?"  "I do,
indeed, sir," said the student, with a frank and

cheerful smile. That, I think, was the only occasion on which anybody ever dared to answer Dill when he was angry. And he could be astonishingly angry, even over such a trifle as a man's taking out his watch towards the end of a lecture. He was a passionate, sensitive man, and an insult whether to scholarship or to the courtesies set him raging like a prophet in a base world.

As a result, one could not sit at ease in his class unless one had a fairly good conscience, and, as he lectured, he made it still more difficult to be comfortable by expecting one to take copious notes. I happen to be one of those people who detest note-taking and can get no good out of a lecture except by listening to it. I did not spoil the effect of any of Dill's lectures by actually taking notes of them, but so commanding was his eye as he gazed round the room that I got into the way of keeping a note-book open before me while he spoke, and filling its pages with the sort of up-and-down scrawls that babies make when they are first given pencils.

The spell of Dill, however, was something more than the spell of awe. He held us in chains of pleasure as well as of obedience. His voice, his presence, his phrasing, his emotional emphasis as he translated a beautiful passage from a chorus, all carried one off into a world in which Æschylus and Sophocles seemed more real than the Lord Mayor of the city. He wore a beard in those days, and, had you met him in Athens over two thousand years ago, you might have mistaken him for Pericles. It was like the ghost of Pericles that his proud, shy figure glided past you in the streets. His very conversation, in its intonation and phrasing, was of such a kind as would have seemed natural in a city that had produced the Platonic Dialogues. He had studied the holy writ of the Greeks till it had entered into his blood and even into his appearance. In the imagination he filled the romantic part of the last of the Hellenes in a modern chimneyed town. He had as little faith in the modern world as it is possible for a man to have. He disliked almost everything in it down to its vocabulary. I remember how he flung the book angrily on his desk when someone, in translating Homer, introduced the word "manure." He denounced the mealy-mouthedness of our generation and bade us read the Bible in search of manlier language. Common-place language seemed at once to hurt and infuriate him as if someone had accidentally spilled boiling water on him. There is a line in Homer which many hopeful young men translate as: "Then we partook of food and drink," and so forth. To use the phrase "partook of" was in Dill's eyes the unpardonable sin against the English language. Again the book would be flung on the desk, and the unfortunate translator would have the enormity of his crime brought home to him till he began to wonder what short of capital punishment could meet the case.

At the same time, these small passions never seemed the passions of a small or finicking man. There was, you could not help feeling, a fire in Dill, burning him up and destroying for him many of the ordinary pleasures of life. He lived for a faith—a faith that was not accepted in the world in which he lived—and it is not a cheerful fate to be the last priest holding a dying taper in the temple of a vanishing religion. Even the Christianity in the world about him seemed to Dill to have decayed. He said to me once that the clergy no longer believe in a future life in the sense in which they once did, immortality was gone as a faith, and that morality was going as a result. Nor did he find any relief from this conviction of decay in laughing irony, as other pessimists have done. He had the gravity of Zeno, and the spectacle of the errors of mortals did not amuse him. I doubt if the world in which he believed ever existed outside a book, and I am not sure that I should be at home in it if it did. But, at least, Dill's faith in it—his mournful backward glances to it as to a holy land—moved the imagination and incited reluctant youth to dive with a new excitement into a difficult chorus of Æschylus, and to listen with a new patience and a new delight to the voice of the dying Socrates. One may have been an idle scholar, but here was a man who made one believe in Athens, its poets and philosophers, as the next most real thing to Belfast and its business men. Only a great teacher can so translate a class-room into a porch of the ideal world.

## The Old Woman Who Lived in a Shoe

THERE recently appeared among the announcements of births in *Le Temps* the following pleasant paragraph:

Jean-Louis, Denise-Madeline et Jean-Claude Bloch ont la joie d'annoncer la naissance de leur frère Jean-Pierre, 6 avenue de Malakoff.

Probably the advertisement was sent in with the collusion, or even on the initiative, of a sentimental parent, though we cannot be sure of this, for some children have an extraordinary gift for managing things for themselves. Whoever may have composed the announcement, it is at least an admirable statement of an eternal truth about human nature. We live in an age of limited families, when men and women are coming more and more to doubt whether a little child is not a great evil. But children themselves are still of the orthodox tradition in the "joy" with which they announce the birth of a new baby. It is true that they show almost equal joy in announcing the birth of a new kitten. They would have congratulated the Old Woman who Lived in a Shoe and would have thought her still happier if she had had not only so many children but so many kittens and so many puppies and so many calves and so many foals and so many chickens and so many ducklings

and so many lambs that she would have been driven
to further and fiercer measures of desperation.
They cannot, fortunately, see the matter from the
Old Woman's point of view. They do not realize
how terrifying is the problem of bringing up a large
family, even in an elastic-sided boot. To them,
indeed, there is no problem except the necessity of
filling the world as full as possible of children, kittens, puppies, calves, foals, chickens, ducklings and
lambs. In this I believe they are æsthetically right.
If children and the young of all animals could be
created by a wish and be fed and housed and made
secure and happy by a wish, how few people there
are who would not create for themselves new Edens
of the young! Most men feel a happiness for which
they could not account at the sight of young animals
—even of young pigs. I will not pretend that a baby
is beautiful on the first day of its birth. Many a man
on being taken in to see his first baby, with its elongated head and its red skin, has an awful moment in
which he silently asks himself: "Is it deformed?"
"My dear boy," a friend of mine said to me, describing his first glimpse of his first baby: "I thought
for a moment I was the father of a monster." No
sooner is it in the cradle, however, than the baby has
admirers at least in other children. Nurses may
play on the jealousy of the older child—a common
phrase is, I believe: "Here's someone to put your
nose out of joint"—but the infant in the cradle is far
too exciting a wonder to be the object of jealousy for
long. I cannot say I am myself an enthusiast for

other people's babies. I am sure that other people, in so far as they are infatuated with them, are happy. But I doubt whether babies in long clothes are fit company for strangers. They are embarrassing except when they are asleep—incapable of conversation themselves and interrupters of the conversation of other people. Provided it is asleep, however, I can feel an extraordinary tenderness for a strange baby in a cradle. I begin even to feel a curious increase of affection for its parents as I look down at its face. There are few more charming spectacles in the world than a night nursery full of children of all shapes and sizes in their cots and cradles. I was shown such a nursery recently, and it seemed as fabulous and bewitching as though it belonged to the fantastic world invented by Sir James Barrie.

Other people's children, however, apart from such agreeable moments for the sentimentalist, are not really attractive until they are able to talk. They need not be able to talk much. If a baby is old enough to pick up a stone with a great effort of stooping and standing erect again, and to toddle across the beach and offer you its treasure, saying the one word, " 'tone," it is already a fascinating conversationalist. Later on, when it has acquired greater strength of limb, it learns to smile as it talks and flatters your vanity by insisting on your watching it perform miracles, such as turning sand out of a bucket or kicking a ball. "Look, Mr. Y., look," cries Stephen. "I'm going to kick the ball right down to the bottom of the path." It is a winding, sloping

path, and Stephen runs at the ball and takes a tre-
mendous kick at it that sends it rolling along the
path at the rate of about a yard a minute. It rolls
down the slope carried by its own weight, and then
nestles into stillness on the grassy verge of the path.
Stephen runs down and retrieves it laughing. In a
minute he has placed the ball for a new kick and is
calling: "Look, Mr. Y., look," with greater excitement than ever. I have never tested myself to see
how long I could enjoy going on looking, for a nurse
invariably comes and carries the child off for a walk
or to play on the beach; but to watch the gambols
of the young is extraordinarily satisfying while it
lasts. At a still later stage, the child's conversation
becomes less openly boastful and more instructive.
The things that small children know about—ants
and green flies and such things—are a continual
source of amazement to me. I generally forget
facts of this kind, and to listen to Ronald on the
subject was as good as reading a book of Fabre's.
Ronald also taught me many things about caterpillars. I suspect, however, that, finding me credu-
lous, he began to pull my leg, for, when I asked him
what certain caterpillars ate, he said, with slow
deliberation: "These caterpillars eat fish-bones—
codfish-bones. First, they eat all the bones up one
side, then they eat through the spine, and then they
eat the bones down the other side." I can believe
almost anything, but, frankly, I found it difficult to
accept Ronald's statement even before he went off
into a long and triumphant chuckle. At the same

time, many of the fanciful perversions of natural
history in which children indulge are matters of good
faith. Young Rupert, for instance, who knows
everything at the age of ten, came up one day to
Charles, who had just captured a quite ordinary
caterpillar. "You should keep that," Rupert told
him, "and it will turn into a chrysalis, and the chrysalis will turn into a moth, and the moth will turn
into a butterfly." "You young ass," said Charles
contemptuously, "don't talk rot. It will do nothing
of the sort." "It will," Rupert assured him ear-
nestly; "all chrysalises turn into moths, and all moths
turn into butterflies." "Don't be an ass," Charles
repeated the insult; "no moth ever turns into a
butterfly." "Well," replied Rupert, doggedly certain that he couldn't be quite wrong, "then butterflies turn into moths." I am afraid that, after that,
Charles began to enjoy laying traps for the omnis-
cient Rupert, not only in natural history, but in all
sorts of things. On the last day of the holiday, all
the children in the hotel sat up for supper, and most
of them had a party at a separate table. Charles
was allowed a bottle of cider in honour of the
occasion. Mice and mumps (to quote a famous
novelist), what cider! A lady who tried a glass of
it said that it tasted as if it had been made from
mouldy apples, and I, who had also tried it, looked
on this description as the grossest flattery. Still,
Charles enjoyed it like a man as he sat at the head of
the table, and, having failed to persuade any of the
girls to take any, offered a glass to Rupert. "Do

you like cider, Rupert?" he asked. "I like all wines,"
young Rupert lied boldly. Charles filled a glass, but
Rupert did not at once drink it. Later, when he
thought no one was looking, he put the glass to his
lips, but even as he swallowed the first mouthful, he
was unable to keep himself from making wry and
sickly faces. Charles's eagle eye was watching him.
"I thought you said you liked cider," he said contemptuously. "So I do," declared Rupert, trying to
keep his face from screwing itself into new distor-
tions; "I like all wines." "Do you like red cider?"
Charles asked him quietly. "Not so much as yellow," said Rupert, "but I like it." "I don't believe
you ever tasted red cider," said Charles, warmly.
"I did—often," lied Rupert, looking as indignant as
he could. "Well, that's where you're caught," said
Charles triumphantly, "for there isn't any red cider."

Yes, the young are unscrupulous, but attractive.
There are few living things, indeed, that are not
infinitely the more charming for being young. The
only things that I can think of which appeal to the
imagination more strongly in their age than in their
infancy are trees. More poems have been written
about old trees than about young ones. It is the
trees most heavily weighted with years that stir our
feelings most profoundly. In most other families of
living things, we are in love with the young, the
irresponsible, the innocent. Our preference, perhaps, has its roots in the eye rather than in the
heart. It is obviously easier to be beautiful as a
child than as a man—as a kitten than as a cat. See

a grown-up cat sitting on a couch, its tail spread out behind it, and its head tilted to one side as it watches a daddy-longlegs dancing in the corner of the ceiling, and it will give you pleasure. But then see the kitten Jeremy taking his place beside the elder cat and, a fifth of the other's size, spreading his tail out in exactly the same curve and tilting his head at exactly the same angle to watch the same daddy-longlegs, and the sight becomes entrancing. Jeremy in his attitude is such a pretty parody—such a reduction of his kind to delicious absurdity. If I had been the Old Woman who Lived in a Shoe, I should certainly have kept kittens as well as children. And ducklings. And, perhaps, young pigs. And I should have hired somebody to look after them all.

## Racing at Dieppe

WHEN I saw that there was to be racing at Dieppe, I knew that, in the American phrase, I was "up against" a temptation that I should be unable to resist. The great merit of horse-racing is that it gives you an excuse for spending an afternoon in the open air, and in the summer of 1924, owing to the unspeakable weather, it was almost impossible to find an excuse for spending an afternoon in the open air. Never have the coasts of England and France been stormier. Never has the sea broken on colder and greyer stones. Hence the crowded condition of the Boule-room at the Casino—that Boule-room so shabby and so stifling compared to the spacious comfort of the Le Touquet tables. I wandered into it because a friend, on leaving France, had bequeathed me a franc with the message that I was to go to the tables and put it on the seven. I can never help believing that a message of this kind means something. I entered the Boule-room in a spirit of childish certainty that I was going to win. I had kept the franc in a separate pocket, and, when I laid it on the seven, it came as a staggering blow to me to hear the man with the ball announcing that the eight had won. I put another franc down on the seven and received another blow. Then another, and another, and another, and an-

other, till I hadn't a franc left in my pocket. Then
I began to play with two-franc pieces, and, in order
to vary the monotony, threw one on to the five. On
this occasion the seven won. I tried the seven
again, and this time the five won. I went on losing
like this till all my two-franc pieces were gone, and
then, with a bitter oath, "Curse Aylwin Pelham
Hereward!"—for it was he who had told me to
back the seven—I rose from the table and hurried
out for a breath of fresh air. A gale was blowing
from the Atlantic, and I was glad of it. I leaned
forward against it, a lone pacer of the shore, for
some time, and meditated on my future line of action.
It may have been the inspiration of the storm, but
I began gradually to feel bolder, and, remembering
that my pocket was still full of five-franc tokens, I
resolved to go in and play, if necessary, till I hadn't
a five-franc piece left. I looked for table number
seven, and I put my token on the seven there. In a
few seconds the croupier was raking it towards him
without pity. I tried other tables and even other
numbers, but, whatever I tried, my little heap of
wealth continued to dwindle till only one piece remained. "That," said I, as I flung it on the seven,
"must be the last." What joy, then, to hear *"Le
sept"* called out as the winning number and to see the
croupier pushing over towards me a little pink
twenty-franc token and three leaden five-franc
pieces! I left my original five francs on the seven,
and *"Le sept"* was announced again. After that I
could hardly help winning, even though another

member of my family kept taking pieces out of my
hand and losing them almost as fast as I made them.
At Boule, if you win once in seven throws, you at
least keep your head above water. After this point
I must have won at least two or three times out of
seven. I had occasional spells of loss that brought
me down to my last five-franc piece again. But I
never staked my last five francs on the seven in vain.
Always it happened that the little heap in my hand
once more increased itself. When at last the
croupier said that his table must close for the afternoon, I staked fearlessly on the seven again and won.
Then he said that the table was *fermé,* but as some
people who had not heard him put on their tokens,
he allowed one more round, and summoning all my
courage, I flung a pink twenty francs on to the seven,
heard the winning call *"Le sept,"* and a pleasant
little heap of a hundred and sixty francs was thrust
towards me over the *baize.* Please do not think I
am boasting. I am merely writing a true story,
which ought to be called *The Vindication of Aylwin
Pelham Hereward.* I trusted him and he did not
betray me. A. P. H.'s franc had multiplied itself
by something like three hundred in the course of two
hours.

Even so, I do not call this a natural way of passing
the time at the seaside. And so, when I read the
posters on the walls announcing the Dieppe races,
I rejoiced at the prospect of a healthier form of
recreation. On Sunday morning the sky was hung
with filthy cotton-wool clouds and it was in vain that

I used my utmost endeavours to persuade either women or children to accompany me from Grande-pluieville to the race-course. I sat down to lunch alone at *La Sole Dieppoise,* poring over a little pink publication called *La Vie Hippique: Guide Préféré des Sportsmen.* Unfortunately, *La Vie Hippique* seemed to be almost entirely concerned with certain races at Deauville, and gave but a line and a half of tips for *Le Meeting de Dieppe.* After lunch I found a motor char-à-banc hanging about outside the railway station with a blackboard that said, *Pour les Courses. 2ff.* There was nobody but a small sandy-haired boy of eight or nine sitting in it and I got in beside him. The conductor and chauffeur both kept shouting *"Pour les Courses"* at the top of their voices, but the passers-by only shook their heads, and we did not get a catch for at least ten minutes, when two girls in their teens climbed smiling into the vehicle. We went on rattling our machinery and yelling *"Pour les Courses"* for several more minutes, but nobody would have anything to do with us and, at last, we set off on a promenade of the streets of Dieppe at a pace something less than that of a garden-slug, calling out *"Pour les Courses"* to the quiet-looking shops that seemed only to want to be left alone to keep the Sabbath. Sometimes we would pull up in order that the conductor might shake hands with a friend and have a brief and apparently amusing conversation. Sometimes we would stop in order that a man in a blue overall might hurry out of a shop and have a brief and

apparently amusing conversation with the chauffeur.
If we paused in a crowded part of the traffic, a
policeman w :uld come up and order us to move on.
If we paused opposite a café a waiter from within
would begin to exchange back-chat with the chauffeur to the great satisfaction of both.  Then suddenly, just as I was beginning to despair of ever
getting to the race-course, the *bourgeoisie* seemed to
spring from the pavement and to take us by storm.
There were *bourgeois* with grey beards, *bourgeois*
with black beards, beardless *bourgeois* with smiles
settled for life under their long pendent noses, a
stout lady who had to be helped in and who still
preserved a belladonna look in the eyes that rolled
above her faded cheeks, two widows funereal in
weepers—as respectable a company, indeed, as any
that ever set on a pilgrimage from Southwark to
Canterbury.  In England, if you go to a race-meeting, you invariably see a number of people you could
not see anywhere else than at a race-meeting, just
as, if you go into a public-house, you see a certain
number of people such as you never see except in a
public-house.  The French have extended the atmosphere of normal life to the café.  It seemed to me,
as I sat among the jolly *bourgeois* and the merry
widows of Dieppe on the char-à-banc, that they had
also extended the atmosphere of ordinary life to the
race-meeting.

It was a curious contrast to one's experience of
race-meetings in England to arrive at the course a
few minutes before the first race, and not to hear

the voice of a single bookmaker disturbing the Sabbath peace. Most of the people present were strolling about—many of them with their families— under the chestnuts at the back of the grandstand, waiting for the names of the starters in the first race to appear on the notice-board. Some of them were in the paddock where a few of the sorriest looking nags I have ever seen were being walked round and round on the grass. The first horse I saw was a chestnut beast with thick knees called My Lord II. I decided to back it, not because I thought it was going to win, but because I had once lost money on a horse called My Lord in England. There was a little row of ticket-offices, most of them ten-franc offices, at which you gave the number of the horse you wished to back and purchased a ticket, as if at a railway station. I confess, when the horses came out on to the course through a crowd of children, most of them looked to me like abdicated 'bus-horses living abroad on a pension. I am, I may say, no judge of horseflesh, but the only animal in the field that looked to me capable of getting over the jumps without dropping dead was a grey animal in blinkers called Gorenflot, and, when the horses can-tered round for the last time, he took the lead to the finishing post so easily that even those who had backed him had hardly the heart to cheer. After the race we all went round behind the stand again to see the prices of the winner and the placed horses going up on the notice-board. Racing in France has this added excitement that no one who has backed

the winner knows how much he has won until several
minutes after the race.  He has to wait on the wet
grass till the clerks have counted the money and
worked out a division sum with the number of the
successful betters as the divisor and the total sum
bet as the dividend.  Then the answer to the sum
appears on the board, looking, as someone said,
rather like a railway time-table.  Gorenflot was,
apparently, a fairly hot favourite, and your ten
francs had turned only into about twenty-two.
Then, if you had backed him, you hurried round
to the rear of the ticket-office at which you had
made your bet and took your place in a queue and in
time drew your money.  I had the pleasure of standing in the queue twice during the afternoon, for I
met some people on the course who knew an owner
and a trainer, and the owner had given them one
winner and the trainer another.  Even so, so cau-
tious a gambler am I that I did not risk more than
ten francs on either of them.  But then I thought
both horses would probably start odds on favourites,
and it is lowering to the spirits to back favourites
even when you know that they are going to win.

How much more amusing it was to back *Soir
d'Avril*, who was number 13 on the card and was the
son of Sea Sick and *Source d'Or!*  He lived up to
his father's rather than to his mother's name, and,
as he hobbled stiffly home on his wooden legs, he
looked as if his proper place would be in a merry-
go-round rather than on a race-course.  In the next
race I again backed number 13, a horse called Bally-

rack, the son of Rackrent and Ballykill. I doubt
if he even started. If he did he must have got lost
on the far side of the course, for I looked for him
in vain among the horses that finished. But there
was at least one race during the afternoon that was
exciting enough to have stirred the blood of the
very spotted cows that grazed in the middle of the
circular course. This was the steeplechase won by
Seddul Bahr, child of Pilliwinkie and Silent Jenny—
a race in which horses lost their riders or fell into
the water as at the Grand National, and a wounded
jockey lay in the ditch unable to rise, and only
hobbled off the course when the stretcher-bearers
arrived and invited him in vain to take his place
on the stretcher. It was not the accidents that made
the race exciting, however, but the beautiful fighting
finish between Seddul Bahr and Samalut. Side by
side they came over the last jump, and then Samalut
shot ahead like a deer and Seddul Bahr seemed to
be left two or three lengths behind. By a desperate
effort Seddul Bahr's jockey, in his blue blouse with
yellow spots, drove him bounding forward till with
a spring he had come level with Samalut. The two
horses charged forward, one jockey lashing at a
shoulder, the other at a loin, and Samalut again got
ahead when Seddul Bahr's jockey seemed to go mad
with new energy, whirled his beast onward till within
ten yards of the post the two horses were neck and
neck, and with a last wave of the arm incited him
to gather all his forces for a superequine leap that
took him past the winning post a nose in front of

the other. How those French men, women, and children shouted! I did not think that I could have had my heart quite so completely in my mouth for so small a sum as ten francs. Then there was the tenterhooks excitement of waiting behind the stand to learn how much we had won, and, men, women, and children, we could have shouted again when we saw that we had won a whole twelve francs. After that we formed once more into quiet little queues outside the pay-boxes—old men, steady-going shop-keepers, discreet shop-girls and widows. I wish Canon Peter Green, who has written so much against betting, had been there. He could not possibly have believed that betting as it is carried on at Dieppe on a Sunday afternoon is a sin. I have seen more unseemly behaviour at a Sunday School *soirée* and more evil passions on the faces of people playing tiddleywinks.

## The Happiest Man on Earth

A WINE and spirit merchant, who died recently, had the forethought to write his own epitaph and to leave instructions in his will that it was to be placed on his tombstone. It was even more flattering than the usual epitaph, as was perhaps to be expected. It ran:

Here lies the remains of G. L. Norris, who lived and died the happiest man on earth, who was always busy doing good and trying to do good, and advising and helping those in trouble. G. L. Norris never knew his advice to go wrong.

How many of us could speak so well of ourselves? How pleasant it must be to be able to look back on one's life and to realize that one "was always busy doing good and trying to do good, and advising and helping those in trouble!" I confess, when I scan my past, I have to search very thoroughly before I can discover even one day on which I was "busy doing good and trying to do good." I can remember several occasions on which I meant to "do good," but something, whether business or pleasure, usually intervened, and I seldom went further in the matter. The truth is, I am so out of practice in this business of "doing good" that I should be hard put to it to tell you what "doing good" is. Was I doing good when I gave that pound, years and years ago, to the Foreign Mission? Or when I gave the two-shilling bit to the Mission for Converting the Jews? Even in these matters I am not sure that I was entirely disinterested, for there was a leading man in the church who, I was told, had begun by saving money as a boy in order to give it to missions, and who was now worth thousands of pounds. Still, parting with the pound—and even with the two-shilling bit—was a wrench, and I see it in the golden light of the past as a reasonably good deed. Even at the present day I cannot bear to hear people attacking missionaries. It may be that, on such occasions something deep down in my subconsciousness whispers: "If missionaries are no good, what about that pound?" Or "If missions are wrong, what about the two shillings you gave to the Jews?" If the attacks on missionaries succeed, one thing is certain. There will have to be deleted from the book of the Recording Angel two entries of some importance:

| Credit Y. Y. | £ | s. | d. |
|---|---|---|---|
| To Foreign Missions | 1 | 0 | 0 |
| To Mission for Converting Jews | 0 | 2 | 0 |

The great thing about contributing money to missions is that it gives virtue a substantial and recognizable form. There are, I believe, various societies of children, such as the Ministering Children's League and, the Boy Scouts, which pledge their members to do at least one kind deed a day. It is not easy to be kind, however, unless you have money in your pocket.  You cannot go about the world smiling at people you do not know and giving them good advice.  There are, I admit, a good many opportunities every day for a negative sort of kindness—the kindness of not losing your temper even with the harmless house-holder to whom your telephone call has been put through by mistake, or, when you yourself have been rung up by mistake, the kindness of not losing your temper with the boor at the other end who impatiently snaps, "Ring off!" How you long to shout back at him, "Swine-hound! You're not fit to be allowed to use a telephone.  Ass, ape, dog-faced baboon!  Go and boil your head." But you say none of these things.  You wearily put back the receiver in its place, and it may be that in preserving silence you have done a good deed.  If you wish to do deeds of a more positive excellence, you will not find it so easy as you think, even in so crowded a city as London.  Begin by offering to carry a lady's bag for her, and see the look of horror she turns on you as if you were a thief.  Offer your seat to an elderly gentleman in a bus, and, as likely as not, he will glare at you in goggling fury, as much as to say, "How dare you mistake a man in the prime of life like me for a helpless old dodderer? Keep your seat, sir.  You need it a deuced sight more than I do?"  That, indeed, was what happened on the last occasion—now some years ago—on which I tried to do a good deed.  On another occasion I tried to interfere in a fight between two drunken boys.  I plunged into the fight and caught one of them by the arm with the result that the other redoubled the fury of his blows and beat the poor fellow about the face till it was one vast bloodstain. Is it any wonder that, for some time past, I have given up trying to do good beyond throwing an occasional penny into the cap of a pavement artist? And I doubt if the Recording Angel enters pennies.

Perhaps there are more opportunities for doing good in a small town like Penarth, where the wine and spirit merchant lived, than in London. He was undoubtedly fortunate in being able to do good with so few ill results that he could immortalize himself on his tombstone as "the happiest man on earth." Was he really so happy as this merely as a result of doing good, or may we not suspect that he owed some of his happiness to his digestion or his friends or his home or his love of reading or of the pictures? Or is it certain that he was happy at all in this super- lative degree? It is not easy to decide whether a man is happy because he thinks he is happy. Hazlitt, whom most people thought embittered and rather miserable, said before he died that he had had a happy life. There is clearly no means of estimating the quantity of a human being's happiness. Looking back, the ordinary man remembers his happy experi- ences more vividly than the pain and wretchedness he has suffered, and he deceives himself into thinking that he has been happier than he really has been. But he cannot measure either his own happiness or his neighbour's. He may know that his neighbour is richer, luckier, healthier, cleverer, more famous than he, but he cannot be sure that this means that his neighbour is happier than he. We do not know for certain even whether an optimist is happier than a pessimist—a laughing philosopher than a weeping philosopher. Each has a different standard of happiness. Pessimists get a great deal of pleasure from the feeling that they are facing the worst that can be known. They exchange the bliss of ignorance for the bliss of knowledge, and they would not change back again. Pessimists as a rule live to a ripe old age. It is questionable if a despairing view of the universe even impairs the digestion as much as a single slice of new bread. The pessimist, indeed, however much he despairs of the universe, seldom despairs of himself, but like the wine and spirit merchant constantly experiences those most exquisite of joys—the joys of self-approval. Most men, it is true, swing like a pendulum between self-approval and self-criticism, but in the moments of self-flattery all are capable of happiness. After all, every man is to some extent a Malvolio, and we sympathize with Malvolio in his punishment largely because we think the punishment excessive for so venial a fault as self-love. Few men have ever lived who did not see themselves greater than they were in the mirrors of their vanity. Even a moralist so free from cynicism as Ruskin held that self-love— "the gratification of our thirst for applause"—is the leading motive of conduct among human beings. "That thirst," he wrote, "if the last infirmity of noble minds, is also the first infirmity of weak ones,

and, on the whole, the strongest impulsive influence
of average humanity: the greatest efforts of the
race have always been traceable to the love of praise,
and its greatest catastrophes to the love of pleasure."
It is difficult to say which is the sweeter—praise from
other people or praise from oneself. Praise from
other people, I fancy, is chiefly valued because few
of us can praise ourselves with confidence unless we
have other people's support. When other people
praise us, they tell us only what we have already
told ourselves, but we may have needed their en-
dorsement in order to be sure that we were not telling lies. The wine and spirit merchant of Penarth
was apparently one of the fortunate few who do not
need the applause of the world in order to be able
to praise themselves with assurance. He described
himself as "the happiest man on earth" as boldly
as a poet of our time has described himself as "the
modern Homer." And yet, for some reason or
other, just as we have remained indifferent to the
claims of "the modern Homer," so we are by no
means convinced that the wine and spirit merchant
was "the happiest man on earth." We can hardly
help suspecting that he thought he was happier than
he was, and that, even when he wrote "G. L. Norris
never knew his advice to go wrong," he was de-
ceiving himself. He "never knew," but we, for our
part, have our doubts. No man is quite so infallible
as to be able to spend his life "advising and helping
those in trouble" without an occasional error.
Even the Delphic oracle only kept its advice from

going wrong by making it so vague that it couldn't go wrong.

Still, a man who writes his own epitaph may be forgiven for trying to cut the best possible figure in it. If you or I had the writing of our epitaphs and were sure that the authorship would never be known, would we be so much more modest than the wine and spirit merchant of Penarth? We, too, would like to inscribe on the tombstone a few sentences that would bid the stranger pause. Epitaphs are notorious liars as it is. If we wrote them for ourselves, would they be any nearer the truth? In this matter I can speak only for myself, but, frankly, I should prefer to be lied about when I am dead. I should like people to believe such pleasant things about me after death that it would be almost impossible for me to recognize my features in the picture they formed of me in their imaginations. Many children, when they fall into a passion, comfort themselves by imagining themselves dead, and a cruel world melted into tears of appreciation when it is too late. To die is to call attention to oneself. The turnkey's son in *Little Dorrit* used to console himself for his miseries in love by imagining himself dead and composing epitaphs for himself before going to sleep at night. How human is the one that begins:

STRANGER
RESPECT THE TOMB OF
JOHN CHIVERY, JUNIOR,
WHO DIED AT AN ADVANCED AGE
NOT NECESSARY TO MENTION.

Here self-love at least makes sure of a prolonged life before retiring into the tomb, an object of respect to passing strangers.

The more we think of ourselves as dead the kindlier our feelings towards ourselves become. We can then deny ourselves nothing. A few poets have written ribald epitaphs on themselves, but they would probably have been angry if such epitaphs had been written on them by anybody else. They were, I suspect, merely inoculating their reputations against disparagement. For the average poet, I am sure, thinks quite as well of himself as the wine and spirit merchant of Penarth. He may admit to a few faults, for he likes to let it be known that he is human, but, being a poet, he is a man of imagination, and sees himself a little larger and nobler than life. He would not dare to say how much larger and nobler. Few men are so honest as the wine and spirit merchant, who has surely written the most genuine, and genuinely egotistic, epitaph since Mr. Thomas Sapsea praised his "reverential wife" in her tomb. *Requiescat in pace!*

## A Sermon on Shaving

NO man can shave every morning for twenty or thirty years without learning something. Even if he is too lazy or too incompetent to shave himself, and submits himself to barbers, he can hardly escape learning something about human nature by the time he is middle-aged. For barbers contain in their ranks every variety of human nature. I have known barbers who were angels; I have known barbers who were devils. Some of them have a touch as light as a falling feather; others wield a razor like a weapon of the stone age, and are not content unless they are allowed to flay as well as to shave you. The latter, I confess, are rare in the more expensive hairdressers' shops; but, if you are economical or poor, and go into one of those little shops in which before the War a shave used to cost three-halfpence, you will in the course of time discover a kind of shaving which makes you feel as if a mob were rushing over your face in hobnailed boots. I do not say that the poor man's barber is always, or even usually, so brutal as this, but undoubtedly the barber whose customers often allow their beards to grow for two or three days at a time gets used to a more determined sweep of the razor in order to clear away so stiff a field of stubble. He cannot suddenly alter his methods for a thin skin that looks as if it scarcely needed to be shaved at all. To such a skin his very shaving-brush feels as if it were made of darning-needles, stabbing the flesh at every touch. His charge is so small that he has no time for the delicacies, and at the end of the shave you find yourself with soap in your nostrils, blood on your jaws, and tears in your eyes. Then you rub into your wounds, so as to make them smart, a piece of alum that has been rubbed into ever so many other wounds, and you wipe your face with a dirty towel that has wiped ever so many other faces. And you come out into the air, glad to be alive and resolving never in future to go to any but the most expensive barbers.

I do not speak as one who is accustomed to being shaved by a barber. I have no longer the courage. In my twenties, however, when I was more indolent, I used constantly to find myself in barber's shops even though, as the razor touched my face, I was not always free from such apprehensive thoughts as: "Suppose the barber should suddenly go mad?" Luckily, the barber never did, but I have known other and comparative perils. There was that little French barber, for instance, who shaved me during a thunderstorm and who sprang into the air at every flash of lightning. There was also the drunken barber who felt for my cheek with the razor as a drunken man reaches out for something and misses it. Having at last brought the razor down on my face, he leaned on it to steady himself, and, by leaning hard, even succeeded in shaving a certain patch

on my right jaw.   I did not dare so much as to utter
a protest while the razor was on my skin.   Even a
whisper, I felt, might unnerve and overbalance the
man, and my jugular would be severed before he
knew he had done it.   No sooner, however, was the
razor temporarily withdrawn from my face—*reculer
pour mieux sauter* is, I think the way the French
describe it—than in a nightmare voice I gasped out:
"No more.   No more.   That will do, thank you."
He looked down at me with stupid, heavy eyes, and
swayed gently with the open razor in his hand.
"You won't say anything to the boss," he said.
"Nasty touch of influenza.   Been trying to cure it.
Get into trouble if you say anything."   I looked at
the razor and spoke, like Harold King of the English, under duress.   "Right," I said.   That happened
a good many years ago, and I am still in doubt
whether I acted as an honourable citizen either in
making or in keeping such a promise.   I was so
exceedingly frightened, however, while the man was
trying to shave me, that I am afraid it never entered
my head to consider my duty as a citizen.   Self-
preservation, they say, is the first law of nature, and
at the moment I cared about nothing except escaping at the earliest posssible moment from that terrible chair.   As I passed out into the street I did
not even mind the fact that a piece of my face was
clean-shaved while the rest of it was not.   I consoled
myself for not reporting the barber with the thought
that, perhaps, he would not have to shave anybody
else that day, that perhaps the next customer would

only want to have his hair cut, and that not very much damage could be done during a hair-cut. Still, these very casuistries show that my conscience was pricking me. It continues to prick me till the present day. Life is full of difficulties if you do not happen to possess the heroic virtues. Never is it more so, believe me, than when you are being shaved by a drunken barber.

It was not, however, perils of this kind—perils, surely, worthy of being added to that catalogue with which Othello used to thrill the ear of Desdemona—that finally decided me never, if I could avoid it, to allow a barber to shave me again. If I now shave myself, it is owing to that middle-aged nervousness which disguises itself in such words as "hygienic." I dislike being touched with shaving-brushes and razors that have been used on other people's faces. I knew a man, who had to grow a beard as the result of a small poisonous cut that he got at a barber's, and I do not wish to have to grow a beard. If one did not mind having a beard, life would obviously be simpler. But most of us, even in these days, would rather do almost anything than grow beards. Much as the average man hates shaving, he hates the notion of growing a beard still more. In this he is entirely unreasonable. He does not know why he dislikes beards any more than he knows why he dislikes medium-boiled eggs. It is clear that a beard is a labour-saving device, but even in an age of labour-saving devices the very laziest of us will have none of it. Again, it is obviously natural to grow a beard, and for a man to shave is to defy nature no less than for a woman to use lip-stick. A beard is also of service in hiding the imperfections of the human face, and a face with an evil mouth and a weak chin may look positively noble in the shelter of a beard. There is, indeed, everything to be said for wearing a beard that could appeal to so slothful and uncomely an animal as man. Yet we go on shaving, and know not why, and if one of our friends appears with two days' growth of beard on his chin, we regard it as evidence of a deficiency in his character. There is an iron law of shaving. You must either not shave at all or you must shave every day. Here there is no room for the moderate man, the lover of compromise, the good-natured being who likes to make the best of both worlds. If you do not shave at all you will be respected. If you shave regularly every morning you will be respected. But if you attempt to strike a nice balance and shave one day and grow a beard another, both camps will combine to denounce you as though you were something unclean. I have never been able to understand why it should be considered unclean to let the beard grow for three days and clean to let it grow for thirty years. There must be some powerful reason why moderation is praised in every other sphere of conduct but is anathematized in this. It is a matter on which I—possessing, as I have said, none of the heroic virtues—bow to public opinion, and I find myself shaving at the mirror every morning as though I were a slave obeying orders. It is a waste of time. I dislike doing it. But if I did not, I should feel an outcast. Shaving is my daily act of hypocrisy. It enables me to feel a better man without being one.

The sermon I wish to preach on shaving, however, is not a sermon against hypocrisy. It is a sermon against putting your trust in any one thing, as though it alone were necessary to perfection, and it came into my head in this way. I bought a safety-razor some years ago, because everybody else seemed to have a safety-razor. For a time it gave me not only the pleasure of a new toy but, I honestly believe, the pleasure of a perfect shave. Months passed, however, and I became dissatisfied. I began to realize that I used to be able to shave better with an ordinary razor. Then I heard somebody saying that, in order to get a good shave, the important thing was not only to have a perfect razor but to have a perfect lather and that So-and-so's soap was the best; and so I went out and bought So-and-so's soap and, for a week or two afterwards, noticed a marked improvement in my morning shave. Once more, in the course of time, I became dissatisfied, and, on this occasion, when I began to attack So-and-so's razor and So-and-so's soap I was told by my friends: "The great thing is to have a perfect shaving-brush." I immediately bought a good shaving-brush, and applied So-and-so's soap according to the directions on the paper that was wrapped round it, moistening the face with cold water before using the soap, and, with the help of So-and-so's

razor, had the first series of satisfactory shaves that
I had had since the War. Were it not for the soap,
even a sharp razor would not give me a perfect
shave. Were it not for the brush, even the soap
would be ineffective. Were it not for the razor, of
what use would the best brush in the world be?
Hence I tell myself: "Do not expect too much from
any one thing." We are always putting our trust in
one thing or another as though it were the key to
perfection, but the truth is we cannot attain to the
inner sanctuary of perfection without a whole bunch
of keys. You would imagine that a perfect shave
was fairly easy of achievement for a serious-minded
man, but it has taken me half a lifetime to discover
the secret of it. The perfect life, or the perfect
State, is probably even more difficult of attainment,
and we make the same mistakes about them, over-
emphasizing the importance of one thing and overlooking the importance of others. We attempt to
save civilization by means of birth control or private
enterprise or Nationalism or Internationalism, as
though any of these things were good in itself except
in company with other equally important things.
The fanatic believes that if he mentions the word
"birth control" or "republicanism" or "communism,"
he has given you the clue to Paradise. But it is
possible to imagine human beings miserable under
birth control, miserable in a republic, and miserable
under the dictatorship of the proletariat. You cannot build a house with only one wall, and you cannot
build a perfect State with only one principle. At

least, so I thought as I soaped my face with perfect soap and a perfect brush, and shaved it with a perfect razor. If there had been such a thing as a golden rule, there would have been no need of Ten Commandments. I am not sure that even ten are not too few. And he who neglects one neglects all. This I said to myself emphatically, dogmatically, this morning, while shaving,

## Seeing the World

I T is surprisingly easy to get out of the habit of
seeing the world. By "seeing the world" I do
not mean sailing in a pirate's junk up the Yoang-ho
or wandering among the South Sea Islands and falling in love with a native princess, or even lecturing
in the United States. I mean going out of town for
a week-end, or, if that is not possible, for a day,
and looking at grass and water and weeds and woods
and wild beasts, such as rabbits and voles and
squirrels. I mean even spending an afternoon in a
country garden where fruit is not sold by the pound,
but grows on trees and bushes. It struck me the
other day that I had not seen a gooseberry growing
on a bush during the present summer, or a straw-
berry in a strawberry-bed, or an apple on a tree
except over a wall in a London suburb. I had been
out of London a good many times, but always to
crowded scenes, and never in the solitude of a wood
or a field or a garden. It must be more than three
months since I listened to a nightingale in Surrey
in a downpour of rain, and, since then, I might as
well have been in prison, for all I have seen of the
full procession of the seasons, with its smells, its
sounds and its colours.

If any fragments of nature have reached me, it

has been for the most part in the form of moths. Every night, as soon as the lights are switched on, moths of all shapes and sizes begin to flutter in at the window, some of them so huge that they seem almost like bats, some of them no larger than a clothes-moth. Noah is said to have taken two of every kind of living thing into the Ark with him. I find it difficult to believe that he took two of every kind of moth.

There are, we are told, more than two thousand species of moths in Great Britain and Ireland alone, and, no doubt, these are only a fraction of the moths that fill the night air of the five continents. Did Noah, I wonder, find room in his Ark for a Dingy Footman or a Dotted Rustic? Did that noble procession up the gangway contain examples of the Lesser Swallow Prominent or the Shoulder-striped Wainscot? Did a Poplar Lutestring or a Setaceous Hebrew Character escape back to the honeyed earth from the bleak scarp of Mount Ararat? Did Noah even know the names that Adam had given all these pretty creatures of the darkness? Adam, it must be confessed, was in a happy mood when he christened the families of the moths. How fancifully he named the members of the Footman family—so called because, when they fold their wings close to their body, they have a "very elongate and stiff appearance!" There are unfortunately only about fifteen kinds of Footman moth in England, but consider the charming list of their names. Among them are:

The Red-necked Footman,
The Rosy Footman,
The Four-dotted Footman,
The Four-spotted Footman,
The Buff Footman,
The Dingy Footman,
The Common Footman,
The Scarce Footman,
The Northern Footman,
The Pigmy Footman,
The Orange Footman.

The suburb in which I live is, I am afraid, too bourgeois to be invaded by creatures of so stiff-backed a dignity. But, when I see a little red-eyed creature making out of the darkness into the lighted room, I always hope that, perhaps, at least, a Dingy Footman, fallen on evil days, may have sought refuge among the houses of the poor. It makes work very difficult if continual broods of unknown moths are coming in through the window all the evening and taking your eyes off your book while you speculate on their names. The longer I live, the less able I am to overcome a childish curiosity to know what things are called, though I have not the patience to learn much more about them and, in a short time, I forget even that. Hence I am always rising from my chair to take down Mr. South's *Moths of the British Isles,* in order to identify that brown creature with a daub of white on its shoulders like a curl of white paint on a palette, that has settled under one of the rings on the yellow curtains. Is it a Silver Y, or a Golden

Y, or any kind of Y at all? It is not at all easy
to identify moths from the illustrations in a book,
because, in a book, all the moths have their wings
spread out like flying butterflies, whereas moths at
rest as a rule fold back their wings into the shape
of a long cloak. The Magpie moth, who has been
our commonest visitor, is luckily recognizable at a
glance by his chequered wings, and a single Magpie
moth flying above one's head is enough to make a
sitting-room alive as a pretty extension of the open
country. Even the kitten becomes excited on seeing
him, and runs about the room in pursuit, leaping
into the air with its forepaws raised, like a Greek
girl playing at ball in a picture. The kitten, indeed,
is still more fascinated by the moths than I am.
His eyes brighten, and his small face goes eagerly
from side to side as he watches the commonest Pug.
I do my best to save the nobler species from him,
such as the Swallow-tail with its fantastic cut-away
wings. But for the most part I have to be content
with the reflection that, even though one moth per-
ishes, there are a hundred as good as he to take his
place. The garden, indeed, has been a brood-farm
of Magpie moths. Their caterpillars feed on the
dull leaves of the euonymus bushes, and their wasp-
coloured chrysalises hang there by the score, awaiting transformation. Strange, I have never been
present at the birth of a moth or a butterfly. Even
if I kept a cocoon in a matchbox in the hope of one
day seeing the miracle of the liberated wings, it
was always sure to be thrown out by tidying hands.

Yet there cannot be many things in nature more wonderful than the escape of a butterfly from its mummy-cloths into the freedom of the air. Alas! if I ever see it, it will probably be on the cinematograph.

Still, for lack of greater closeness to nature, it is very pleasant to be surrounded at one's work by moths and flies and butterflies already full-grown. There is the Lacewing fly, with long, transparent green wings of an exquisite network, and long waving antennæ, which is said to prey upon baser insects. He was still in the corner of the window-frame this morning. There is the Mottled Beauty. There is— But there are more moths on the windows and ceilings than you would see in a collector's case. I cannot discover even the names of most. I can but look at one of them and see in the markings of his folded wings the image of the face of an anonymous Maori god.

These things, however, seem most charming in contrast to walls and streets. You have only to take a train a few miles up the river in order to find a world better worth looking at than a ceiling of moths. You can see most of the things that are best worth seeing in the world from the floor of a punt. I do not know how much the punter himself sees, for I have not the figure for that kind of employment. I experimented with the pole but for a few minutes, and then behind the concealment of an island, but it was enough to show me that the difficulty of reaching the bottom of the river with the pole, and of recovering both the pole and one's balance while striking a really effective blow at the mud, was a problem for subtler heads than mine. Besides, just as I was turning the punt round, spectators arrived. The punt was as obstinate as a mule, and, the more the spectators looked, the more obstinate it became.

The inhabitants of the river are polite, but the stare of their languid and curious eyes is embarrassing. Only a few minutes before, I had been admiring the tall white-trousered figure of a youth, as it gracefully stooped towards the water and gracefully straightened itself again, pole shooting into the air, for another thrust into the stream. With what delicious ease the punt moved through the still water, over mirrored cloud and sky and willow! With what arrowy straightness! I must have hallucinated myself into the thought that I, too, might be just such an Olympic figure, guiding my little bark up the stream with calm and magisterial muscles. Had I been in a tub, however, I could not have felt less like one of the early gods. Not only did I get wet myself, but I made other people wet, and one more dream burst into fragments like a broken glass. There are some people whom it suits to stand on the stern of a punt and punt. There are others whom it suits to lie among the cushions in the hollow of a punt and be punted. This has all the appearance of a lazy life, but at least the eyes are not lazy as you glide past the jungle of the banks and see the coloured flowers reflected in the stream.

Here was the full garden of summer—purple loose-strife and willow-herb and campion growing larger than life out of the mud—a forest of August flowers above floating yellow water-lily and arrow-head. Occasionally, another punt passed, with the clothes of campers-out hanging on a line and a gramophone playing fox-trot after fox-trot at the bidding of an idle girl. But most of the punts and skiffs and canoes that one met seemed but part of the peace of the river—almost as much as the dragonflies, brilliant as peacocks, that darted out from the bulrushes over the water. White clouds in the sky, white clouds in the water, beechwoods if you looked up, beechwoods if you looked down, iris-leaves and flowers in the air, iris-leaves and flowers in the stream—a world at peace, and the shadow of a world at peace—there was seldom any ruder interruption of the stillness than the splash of a jumping fish or the cry of a moorhen. There is always an element of the incredible in such a scene to anyone who has been living the settled life of a townsman. He can scarcely believe it is true, even when he lands on an island and is bitten by insects and eats cold chicken and hears the cork of a claret-bottle being drawn. How cheerful it was to reflect that I might have been at the big fight at the Stadium and was here among the dipping swallows and the water-lilies instead! It is true that when I declined to go to the fight I did so because I had so much work to do. But the river was a temptation beyond my powers of resisting. "I will do twice as much

work on Sunday," I told myself, and, leaving my conscience in London, I was here watching the bronze,
inquisitive neck of a dabchick, as it bobbed on the
water like a thing of India rubber and sought refuge
by diving among the reflections. "It strikes me,"
said a ferryman later in the afternoon, "that the
river's about done." He longed for the return
of the crowds of boats that used to moor under
his tea-garden. Looking at the river from a different point of view, I could not agree with him.

To advance into this summer solitude, with a
green hill seen above a bend in the river—to see
the world changing before one's eyes like a dream
as one went on—to smell the strange smell of water
—to lie on one's back in the sun—this is all that
most of us who do not possess a tea-garden ask of
the river, and we cannot think of this heavenly solitude as a wilderness.

## On Going Abroad

THE worst of going abroad is that the feeling of being abroad does not last beyond a few days unless one goes still further abroad to a new place. How exciting is the first day in Dieppe, with houses of a different shape and a different colour from the houses to which one is accustomed and with the names and the trades of the shopkeepers all seeming novel and fantastical! How much more charming still is Italy, with the shop fronts painted all over with words ending in *o* and *ia* and *a!* Even such a word as *bottiglieria* seems to speak of a wine-bar in wonderland, and every jeweller's and haberdasher's and silk-merchant's gives as much pleasure to the fancy as if it were a shop discovered under the ocean with a merman for shopwalker and a concourse of mermaids serving at the counters. The look on the streets is so strange that one walks through them with a kind of secret smile. The policemen are different. The cabs are different. The boys selling lottery-tickets on the pavements, the Fascisti lurching along in their black shirts, the monks in their sandals, are all figures that break in with the effect of surprise on common experience, and for a few days one almost mistakes novelty for Paradise. For a few days one even finds oneself assiduously going into churches in a

spirit of exaltation simply because they are not the
churches of the city in which one lives. As for the
food, how charming, if it is edible, is the first meal
after one's arrival in a strange town! I confess I
am incapable of criticising the food in a foreign
country—always excepting such dishes as boiled
mussels, braised lettuces, etc.—for twenty-four
hours after arrival. Even the *vin ordinaire*—which,
to be quite honest, is usually no better than the ordinary wine at an English wine-merchant's—seems
worth a compliment at the first two meals, and, if
one is of romantic disposition, it may be a month
or more before one discovers how bad it is. Time
passes, however, and, even though abroad, we begin
to feel at home. Things no longer please us merely
because they are novel. We pass the shops with as
little interest as if they bore above their windows
such accustomed inscriptions as "Family Butcher,"
"Stationer," or "Italian Warehouseman." We
cease to notice that the policemen look different
from any other policemen. The trams no longer
excite us by their unusual colour and design. The
streets become our familiar walks. We find it
extraordinarily easy to pass a church without going
inside. The flavour of the food becomes monotonous. Our palate recovers its rectitude and becomes critical of the wines. We realize that we
were the victims of an illusion and that we could
have preserved the illusion only by going further
and reviving it in another country or, at least, in
another town. I am not sure that the illusion is

worth having at the price, but many men have become nomads in pursuit of it, travelling from country to country as though no country could be delightful after it was known. They are lovers of the surface, easily enamoured of many places, but passionately in love with none. They hanker after China and Arabia, because they were not born there. If they had been born in China or Arabia, they would have hankered after England and a weekend at Brighton would have seemed to them like an episode in a legend. A great deal of travel, indeed, is little more than restlessness—a continual pursuit of novelty of sensation—and springs from the dread of the boredom of custom. It is as if a man wished to sit on a painted horse—and on a new kind of painted horse every day—in a perpetual merry-go-round.

There are, I know, profounder pleasures to be got later on from foreign places than these superficial excitements over novelties. But they are the same pleasures in kind that are to be had at home. The senses are no longer the supreme means of enjoyment, but the affections are engaged, and we love the things around us all the more because they are familiar. We no longer live in obedience to a guide-book, but have made a new map of the place for ourselves in which many sights that the guide-book exalts are left out and many things not mentioned in the guide-book stand out as prominently as museums and cathedrals. Not that I would speak ill of guide-books. I cannot comfortably go about

with one in my hand or consult it in public with eyes
that glance backwards and forwards between the
book and some ruined temple or great man's tomb.
But I like to have one by me for an occasional private hint, and I like, on getting back to the hotel
after a morning spent in sight-seeing, to take up the
guide-book and see what I have seen, and also what
I have missed. I feel a little humiliated if, after
having gone half across Europe and spent a morning in one of the show-places of the world, I have
on coming home to answer "No" to the questions:
"Did you see this?" "Did you find that?" "Did
you notice that wonderful so-and-so? Oh, what a
pity! It's the gem of the whole place." The guide-
book judiciously studied will save you from many
of these humiliations, though not from all, for the
ordinary traveller is a jealous being and will not be
content till he has proved that you have overlooked
the thing without parallel—that, if you have seen
the right picture, you have seen it in the wrong light
by going in the afternoon instead of the morning—
that your day spent in visiting some famous church
was wasted because you didn't see the cloisters, as
the cloisters are the only thing that raises it above
fifty other churches of the same kind. So far as I
can judge, it is the object of many travellers to con-
vince some poor fellow-creature just returned from
abroad that he might as well have stayed at home,
and that he has not used any of his opportunities
They even try to prove that you have eaten in the
wrong restaurants, taken the wrong guide-book,

and stayed at the wrong hotel. They beam with a horrible philanthropy as they condole with you over what you have missed. But you know all the time that they are secretly enjoying your poverty of experience and congratulating themselves on their own riches. When I was younger, and bolder than I am now, I could have stood up to these people better, and told them with half-truth that I hate sight-seeing, and that, of the famous sights that I have seen, not more than half have given me more pleasure than I could get in a London teashop. I have now a sort of cowardly longing to see everything that everybody talks about, though the pleasure of seeing many of these things is little more than the pleasure of curiosity satisfied. The trouble is that the imagination is not a slave that will take orders from us and that will respond as it is expected to respond at all times and in all places. We go in its company to see a great picture, and stand waiting for its verdict. If we held a dialogue with it, we should say on many such occasions: "Come now. This is one of the great pictures of the world. Everybody says so. At least, everybody says so except the people who always contradict what everybody says. Don't you admire it, too? You don't seem very enthusiastic. Don't you think it very good?" And the imagination would—at least, now and then—reply: "I don't know whether it's good or not, and to-day I don't care. You dragged me here against my will, when I would rather you had sat down in a chair outside a café and watched the buses passing. Besides, picture-galleries always de-press me. The human beings in them never look natural. Many of them look like uneasy ghosts that have wandered into the wrong hell. The ones that are enjoying themselves and expressing their enjoyment aloud are still more disturbing. I can't help listening to them, and one cannot be absorbed in the conversation of one's fellow-creatures and in the Holy Family at the same time. If you had brought me here yesterday, I might have felt dif-ferently, so I shan't go so far as to say that the pic-ture is positively bad. But to-day I simply don't enjoy looking at it. Don't let's bother any more about pictures to-day. Come along to a café." And how gladly we should go!

When once you have settled down and feel really at home in a new place, you need no longer drag your imagination about in this fashion, seeing the things you ought to see instead of the things you wish to see. The resident alien in London does not visit Westminster Abbey with a guide-book, nor does he even go into the National Gallery except when it is the whim of his imagination to do so. If he likes London, it is not because of the things that are marked as important in the guide-books about London. It is because of the things that he discovers capriciously and by accident. He can live in his own London, not in other people's London. London becomes to him a city of personal associa-tions and is no longer a mere capital of famous sights. We are sometimes told that the American

visitor sees more of London than the people who
live in it. This, I think, is true only in a superficial
sense. The American sees more of guide-book London, but the Londoner sees more of the London
that is worth seeing. He sees his own house and
his friends' houses—buildings that contain far more
of the things that make life interesting to him than
cathedrals and palaces and museums of the arts.
He sees his own garden, which contains more pleasures for him than the greatest of the parks, and he
sees his own cat, which surpasses the King's horses
or the lordliest beast in the Zoo as the paragon of
animals. And do not think that he does not see as
many novelties as if he were taxi-ing from church
to church and from museum to museum in a foreign
city. The seasons alone should give a man all the
novelties he needs. The very street in which he
lives changes from hour to hour. It is one street
when the sun is shining, another street in rain, and
another under the full moon. Foreign travel is
pleasant chiefly because it makes us realize that
we are among novelties, but when we are sufficiently
awake to see the constant flow of novelties in the
world at our doors, we can enjoy all the excitement of foreign travel along with the pleasure of
being at home. The worst of it is that, though I
know this, I also know that if I had a fortune I
should spend some of it in Florence, and a little in
Assisi, and might even be tempted as far as Athens.
But no further. I don't mind reading about the
ends of the earth in fiction or in travel-books, but

I trust that, if I ever see them, it will be many years hence and from a window in Heaven. If I were offered a free trip round the world, I might accept the offer through weakness, but I do not wish to go round the world. Have I not been round the sun once a year ever since I was born? That seems to have satisfied any cravings I may have had for distant travel, or at least to have made a jaunt round this pigmy earth a matter of small consequence. Besides, I should hate to meet all those people who are described in the books by anthropologists. I would far rather go to Southend than to the South Seas. And I don't very much want to go to Southend.

## An Academy of Superstitions

ENGLAND is such a disorderly country that it does not even possess a written constitution. It is a country with one of the greatest languages in the history of mankind, but it is too anarchistic to appoint an official guardian of its language, as the French have done for theirs, and leaves us at the mercy of privately-published dictionaries when we are in doubt as to the spelling or pronunciation of a word. The dictionaries unfortunately differ, some of them yielding to a mis-pronunciation that has become general, and some of them holding conservatively fast to the best traditions of speech. Thus you will find varying pronunciations of such words as "corollary" and "laboratory" from dictionary to dictionary, and the influx of American dictionaries has added to the confusion with alternative pronunciations of "metallurgy," schedule" and a host of other words. Even so, I should regret to see the English language made subject to a body of official persons. We saw how the French Academy refused the other day to admit the useful word, *défaitisme,* to the dictionary, and in English academic circles, no doubt, official bias would play as dangerous a part in the selection and rejection of new words. It is better, perhaps, to leave the English language as a tree of the forest instead of trying to clip it into an orderly and unnatural shape, like a sculptured yew-tree.

There is one sphere of English life, however, in which I think an academy might prove extremely useful. I should like to see an Academy of Superstitions established for the classification and, as it were, hall-marking of superstitions. At present the superstitions of western Europe are in such a chaotic state that none of us quite knows what to believe. We are at the mercy of any novelty of belief that is mentioned in casual conversation, and have no guidance in the matter except what we can get from absurd books of dreams and omens. A fellow guest at luncheon, refusing celery, says: "No, thank you. I never eat celery on Tuesday. It's said to be unlucky," and, immediately we make a note of his ridiculous whim and we know that we shall never enjoy eating celery on Tuesday again. Then there is a widespread disagreement about the validity even of some of the most popular superstitions. Most of us, for instance, regard it as unlucky to light three cigarettes from one match. There is a vigorous minority, however, which protests that this is not a genuine superstition, but that it was put about during recent years by a leading firm of manufacturers of matches. Others declare that it originated during the Boer War, when it was noticed that, if a match was kept alive long enough to light three cigarettes, a Boer sniper frequently fired at the light and shot one of the three smokers. These rationalists admit that the superstition is valid enough in time of war, but deny that it has any force in time of peace. This is an example of the sort of difficulty that an Academy of Superstitions ought to be able to clear up once and for all. It could inquire into the origin of the superstition, subpœna the heads of the firm of manufacturers of matches, compile statistics showing the effect of economy in matches (*a*) during peace and (*b*) during war, and either perpetuate the superstition as a good one or decree its expulsion for ever from the company of reasonable men. As it is, those of us who do not like to run unnecessary risks have to be constantly on our guard against hosts who do not care what happens to us.

Then there is the superstition which forbids us to walk under a ladder. Most of us accept this without question, though a number of people who like to make the best of both worlds invariably explain that the reason why they do not like walking under ladders is that they are afraid of somebody dropping a pot of paint on them. I find, however, from a book, *Lucky Charms and Omens —What They Mean,* that the only time it is safe to walk under a ladder is when there is somebody on it. "It is very unlucky to walk under a ladder," says this little volume, "unless there is a man on it, when it becomes quite a fortunate thing to do." I confess I had never heard of this reservation before, and I should like to know what authority the editor of the book has for it. Obviously, if he is right, one's attitude to ladders will have to undergo serious alteration. I myself, for instance, am willing **to**

risk a pot of paint in the pursuit of good fortune,
and I am sure there are hundreds of other bold
spirits who will be willing to encounter the same
perils in so good a cause. But, for want of official
guidance, we are at a loss what to believe. We do
not know whether the theory just mentioned is in
accordance with tradition or is a frivolous invention of recent times. If an Academy of Superstitions were in existence, and publicly announced that
the superstition about the ladder with a man on it
could be traced back to the Middle Ages, it would
do much to set our doubts at rest and would add
considerably to the happiness of those of us who
have to walk a great deal in the streets.

During the past summer I came on yet another
example of the confusion into which superstitions
have fallen in modern days. I happened to be in
Pourville with nothing to do, on a dismal Sunday
afternoon. A barber's shop was temptingly open,
and, as I had long been meditating a visit to the
barber's, I should undoubtedly have gone in as a
relief from the murky sky, if an old superstition had
not suddenly come into my mind. I remembered
that it was unlucky to cut one's nails on Sunday, and
took it for granted that the omen applied equally to
hair. When I got back to the hotel, I was describing the miseries of the afternoon and how, by a
happy stroke of luck, I had been saved from adding
to them by having my hair cut on a Sunday. "Oh, but
didn't you know?" a lady interrupted me, and she
quoted what she alleged to be an old saying: "Who

cuts his hair on Sunday, cuts it to the glory of God."
Now, I had never heard the old saying before, and
you can imagine what a blow it was to learn of
the golden opportunity I had missed. I straight-
way added a belief in Sunday hair-cutting to the
list of my superstitions, and it has remained there
until the present week. During the week, however,
I have been reading *Lucky Charms and Omens*,
which tells me that "Fridays and Sundays are considered lucky days on which to tell one's fortune,
but not for cutting hair or nails." Whom am I to
believe—the lady or the editor? The lady's proverb had a traditional air about it, and it is difficult
to believe that she invented it on the spur of the
moment merely in order to give pain. If I were a
Gallio, who could achieve an attitude of cold-
blooded indifference on such matters, I should be
able to laugh both at the lady and the editor. But,
as it is, I am simply bewildered and do not know
where to look for guidance.

It is the custom to speak of "these enlightened
days," but, in these enlightened days, those of us
who are superstitious are no better than sheep without a shepherd. We live in a thick fog of ignorance,
as impenetrable as it can ever have been in the
Dark Ages. Our age has thrown light on many a
branch of the tree of knowledge, but, when we advance into the jungle of superstition, we find ourselves surrounded by a secular darkness in which it
is impossible to distinguish between nourishing fruit
and poisonous berries. It surely provides a melan-

choly comment on a so-called age of enlightenment
that no illuminating ray has ever penetrated into so
important a part of our lives as our superstitions.
So far as they are concerned, we might as well be
living under William Rufus. Add to this the fact
that, in an age in which we have been able to invent
a counter to almost every danger (so that we have
already a defence against terrors so modern as air-
craft and submarines), most of us are as yet as
ignorant as savages of the means of averting ill-
luck. Yet I am confident that there is not a single
evil omen that cannot be turned into a good one by
the cunning of mankind. *Lucky Charms and Omens*
tells us, indeed, that a means is already known of
counteracting misfortune for those who are unlucky
enough to see a single magpie flying. "If," it de-
clares, "you turn round once—left wheel, not cart-
wheel!—you avert misfortune." Unhappily, it is
often from the window of a railway carriage that
one sees a single magpie, and it is not easy to perform a sudden left-wheel turn in a crowded railway
carriage without attracting more attention than the
ordinary man desires. An Academy of Superstitions would be invaluable in devising counter-charms
more suitable to the conditions of modern life.
Even the action of throwing over one's left shoulder a pinch of the salt that one has spilt is too public
to be entirely pleasant at a dinner-party. I should
like the Academy of Superstitions to invent a number of verbal charms that one could mumble under
one's breath without being noticed. There are

already, I believe, many such charms in existence.
I have heard a horoscopist, as he passed under a
ladder, muttering some kind of trigonometrical
formula, and I understood that it was perfectly effective. I should like some charm of the same kind
as an alternative to such things as picking up pins,
which is becoming quite intolerable as a means of
obtaining good fortune in so pin-bestrewn a city as
London. From sheer weariness, I have long since
ceased to look at the pavement. But at times the
eye wanders. One may even see a pin on the rail-
way-line from the platform of a tube station, and
what is one to do then? If there were a verbal
charm for the occasion, one would feel more comfortable. In the absence of such a charm, one can
but stare at the pin with a sinking feeling at the
heart.

If the Academy of Superstitions is ever established—and, if it is, I suggest that it should con-
sist of twelve men, say, the Archbishop of Canterbury, the Moderator of the General Assembly of
the Church of Scotland, the Poet-Laureate, the
Home Secretary, Sir Arthur Conan Doyle, Father
Ronald Knox, the President of the Rational Press
Association, Mr. David Kirkwood, Lord Banbury,
the head of the Air Force, the oldest inhabitant in
Devonshire, and almost any Irishman—it is clear
that it will have a programme of work that will
keep it busy for many years to come. It will, I trust,
in addition to its many other duties, ruthlessly exam-
ine all the superstitions that are brought to its notice,

and feel not the slightest scruple about abolishing any superstition which seems to it ridiculous or insufficiently supported by the experience of the human race. For instance, I should like to have its report on the superstition, referred to in *Lucky Charms and Omens,* that "it is very, very lucky to touch a real sailor's blue collar with the white braid on it." Until I have the authority of the Academy for ignoring this superstition, I shall find it difficult not to accost every sailor I meet and to lay my forefinger on his blue collar, though I know that sailors are, for the most part, pugnacious and irascible men. Again, I should be glad of an authoritative ruling on the genuineness of the superstition that "it is considered an omen of ill to sell a piebald horse," and of the, to me, equally novel superstition that "if you wish when passing a farm, and if you see a pig before you have passed the steading, you will obtain your wish." Until such a ruling has been made public, I can scarcely imagine myself selling a piebald horse, and I fear that most of my country walks will be taken up with the search of pigs round farmhouses. There is another curious superstition mentioned in the book. "Horses," it says, "are mostly lucky." All I can say on this point is that thousands of Englishmen have not found them so. The Academy of Superstitions will confer a great benefit on a large and deserving section of the community if it can either expose this superstition as a common delusion or devise some means of making horses as lucky as most of us would like them to be.

Here, then, is something that Mr. Baldwin's government can set about doing at once. Mr. Baldwin is said to be in difficulties about a constructive programme. Let him establish the Academy of Superstitions in the next session of his Parliament. He might even have a Minister of Superstitions in the Cabinet. After all, he is the head of a party which has always thrived on superstitions, and even to-day certain superstitions about the colour red are more useful to the party than any other item in its creed. But *Lucky Charms and Omens* does not agree with Mr. Baldwin about colours. It says: "One is said to be in the best of health, if one wants to wear anything red,"

# The Plasterer's Arms

THERE is a curious notice hung outside a public-house in Seymour Street near Euston Station. The name of the public-house itself, "The Plasterers' Arms," is curious enough, but I like better still the warning notice suspended outside, which runs: "The last public-house before reaching the Strand—1¼ miles." I have never been inside "The Plasterers' Arms," for I am usually on the top of a bus when I am in the neighbourhood. But, even when I am on foot, I can read the notice dispassionately enough and pass on. How many men are there, I wonder, who have been tempted to go in by the reminder that, if they do not have a drink here and now, it will be in vain to look for one till they have reached the end of the long desert that begins at Euston Road and ends just opposite the office of the *Morning Post?* "Can I hold out?" the stranger from the north asks himself on catching sight of the fatal words and, as he does, the mile and a quarter stretches out in his imagination till it seems to run half-way across Africa. In ordinary life, it is quite a common experience to walk a mile and a quarter without going into a public-house. But, if you are a stranger in a great city and want to rest the soles of your feet while washing the dust out of your throat, it is extraordinary

how long even half a mile seems if there is no
"Angel" or "Green Dragon" to be seen anywhere
guarding a street-corner. Then there is the noble
company of the pub-crawlers who pass from tavern
to tavern in the course of an evening as we pass
from birthday to birthday in the course of a lifetime. They, too, will be aware of a strange emotion as they read the sign of "The Plasterers'
Arms." For them the perfect world would be
a world dotted with public-houses at every hundred
yards. They like just enough fresh air to blow the
fumes out of the brain, just enough exercise to settle
the last half-pint or the last whiskey-and-soda into
position well under the heart. They are not nature-
lovers or athletes that they can face the prospect
of longer walks with equanimity. They are men who,
if they go to Brighton, have a drink at the station
lest there should be no public-houses on the front,
and have a drink on the front lest there should be
no bar on the pier, and have a drink on the pier out
of sheer joy at finding there is a bar on the pier after
all, and then go back to the front for another drink
because they like a change. Such is one of the
many human devices to avoid monotony. After all,
there is as much monotony in the drinks themselves
as any man could endure, and the only chance of
variety is in continual change of place—from the
"Dog and Duck" to the "Green Man," and then,
after a look in at the "King of Bohemia," on by
way of the "Holly Bush" to the "Seven Stars," not
forgetting to drop in at the "Camel's Hump," where

some of the boys are in great spirits and are singing
"Do have a tiddley at the fountain" to a hymn-tune,
and so on to the "Spread Eagle," the "Slip Inn,"
the "Gospel Oak," and the "Singing Hen," with
just one more or, if there is time, two to end up with
at the "Midnight Sun." Did Livingstone himself
ever set forth on such travels?

I fear that pub-crawlers of this type are not so
common as they used to be. Most of them have
perished, having been either run over by motor-
buses on their way home or reformed by age or
even terrorized into temperance by the high price
of post-war liquor. No doubt, they felt that they
had lived on into an age that had little sympathy
with their foibles. All the world seemed to be mar-
shalled in hostility against them. Many publicans
would give them only bad liquor, and an increasing
number of people wanted to give them no liquor
at all. Only the bravest idealists could have carried
on the battle in face of such universal discouragement, but pub-crawlers held their banner aloft gal-
lantly enough till they fell in the last ditch in our
own time. Those who survive seem lonely and
melancholy figures—blear-eyed brothers of the
Wandering Jew.

I hope "The Plasterers' Arms" will still continue
to display its kindly notice, so that succeeding ages
may realize something of the difficulties men had
to contend with in the early days of the nineteenth
century. There was a similar notice, I am told, outside a public-house near the Queen's Club athletic

ground, which ran: "No other public-house for half
a mile." How desolate a half-mile that must have
seemed to many a reader of the words! Yet, in
spite of the evidence that even a single half-mile
becomes a desolation and a desert in such circumstances, there are people who would gladly see the
whole of London turned into a Sahara with the last
"White Swan" singing her dying-song to the parched
inhabitants. The world is in a curious state.
Everybody believes in temperance spelt with a rea-
sonable-sized "t"; but the people who believe in it
most strongly believe in Temperance spelt with a
capital "T," or rather they believe in Teetotalism,
which is Temperance spelt with two capital "T's."
Any school child who spelt Temperance with two
"T's" would be justly reproved by its teachers, but
eminent men and women can misspell the word as
they please amid the applause of their followers.
For such as they there is no pathos in the words,
"The last public-house before reaching the Strand—
1¼ miles." Some of them would even say, "Jolly
good thing. I only wish it were 10¼ miles." Look
how in recent years they have treated the *bona-fide*
traveller. In my youth, a man was considered a
*bona-fide* traveller if he had travelled three miles,
and all public-houses were open to him even during
closing hours. He was not a traveller, perhaps, in
the sense in which Mr. Cunninghame Graham is a
traveller, but no one questioned the *bona fides* with
which he set out on his journey and, if his object
was a public-house rather than the North Pole or

some lost city in central Africa, that was his affair. Then the law decided that a three-mile bus-ride did not give a man the right to be counted the peer of Marco Polo and Mary Kingsley and C. M. Doughty. He was now compelled, as evidence of his good faith on a Sunday afternoon, to travel at least five miles. He rose to the situation like a man, and travellers from Hampstead went all the way to Richmond with the light of *bona fides* in their eyes and Richmond men with a thirst for travel went all the way to Hampstead. This, instead of satisfying the reformers that a genuine love of travel was widespread among Englishmen—as, indeed, they might have guessed, for are not the English an Imperial race?—seems only to have distressed them and they took the first opportunity to strike such a blow at the love of travel as had never been known in history. They abolished *bona-fide* travel altogether, so that now there is no inducement for the Hampstead man to leave Hampstead on a Sunday at all or for the Richmond man to leave Richmond.

Those who are so much out of sympathy with the common instincts of mankind that they would prohibit travel itself as a vice—prohibit the only kind of travel, indeed, that has ever been officially recognized as *bona-fide* travel by kings and parliaments—cannot be expected to be interested in asking themselves why their fellow-creatures should respond in great numbers or in small to the appeal of those words, "The last public-house before reaching the

Strand—1¼ miles." Yet it seems to me that the
words appeal to something permanent and almost
universal in our nature. They appeal not only to a
natural physical thirst but to our love of the last
chance and our fear of missing it. For some reason
or other, we set a special value on things if we know
that this will be our last chance of enjoying them.
With what excitement we crowd to a concert-hall
at which a great singer is about to make his last appearance in public! How eagerly we book our seats
to see a Coquelin or a Duse if we have the feeling
that we shall never be able to see him or her again,
and that this is our last chance! Advertisers and
auctioneers play upon this weakness of ours, and
are never more effective than when they seem to be
saying to us: "Hurry up, this is your last chance,"
and, indeed, the last pause of the auctioneer's ham-
mer on the eve of "Gone!" must have tempted many
a man to bid high for an object that he would never
have dreamed of buying if he had seen it in a shop-
window and expected it to stay there. Evangelists,
too, excite their audiences by suggesting to them
that to-morrow may be too late and that, if they
miss the opportunity of salvation to-day, they will
miss it for ever. Even the Epicureans, with their
*Carpe diem,* get round us by persuading us that life
is a series of last chances of happiness, and that we
must seize them now if we are to seize them at all.
All the world, whether it is exciting us to good or to
evil, seems to cry, "Do not delay. This chance may
never recur again." No one has ever spoken a

good word for dilatoriness, which is an optimistic
attitude due to the belief that, rich as to-day is in
opportunities, to-morrow will be richer. "The
Plasterers' Arms," like the Dean of St. Paul's,
sternly summons us from such benevolent lethargy,
and attempts to convert us to a reasonable and realistic pessimism. If a man gaily sets out from Euston
Road, believing that he will easily find a public-
house somewhere between that and the Strand, it
warns him that he is labouring under a delusion.
Hotel-bars and restaurant-bars he may find, but, as
for public-houses, they are as rare along that route
as they are, according to the Salvation Army hymn,
in Heaven. Why, then, not make a call at "The
Plasterers' Arms?" It is your last chance till you
reach the Strand, and, in the present state of the
licensing laws, the public-house in the Strand may
be closed by the time you get there. All nature
cries, "Do it now." There are few sadder words
in the English language than "Time, gentlemen,
please!" The sign of "The Plasterers' Arms" is a
subtle variation on that ancient theme. If Omar
Khayyám had seen that sign, do you think he could
have remained outside? I don't.

## The Money-Lenders

IT is, I suppose, a fact that far more people have suffered at the hands of money-borrowers than of money-lenders. Yet it is the money-lender and not the money-borrower whose activities we are always denouncing and trying to curb. I doubt if there is a single law in existence against borrowing money. If there is, I have never heard of its being enforced. I have borrowed money so often myself that I do not complain of this, but I should like to see it made an offence against the law to borrow money from a person you have never seen before. When I was younger, it was a common enough thing for a perfect stranger who had somehow or other got hold of one's name to call in at the office and announce that he had just been given an excellent job in a town in the far north of England, and that, if one lent him his railway fare, he would be a made man for life. In youth one has an ardent faith in people with good jobs waiting for them in northern towns who are so friendless that they have to borrow the railway-fare from someone whom they have never met before. I have long since lost that faith, for never once did I receive so much as a post-card from the north of England explaining that, though the job was a good one, it would take

years to save enough money to repay the price of
the railway-ticket. That indeed, was all I hoped
for. I wanted to be sure that the man had really
gone to the north of England. One does not feel
foolish for having lent money that will never be
paid back, but one does feel foolish if one has lent
it for one purpose and if it is spent on another. Is
there not a story of Addison's lending Steele some
money to pay the rent, and of his anger on finding
that Steele had laid it out on a drinking-party? So
far as I can remember the story, Addison, in his
wrath at being fooled, had Steele put under arrest.
I should not like to proceed so far against the men
who borrow the fare for imaginary railway-jour-
neys. But I resent the fraud on my sentimentality.
Yet I must in honesty confess that, if they had not
told the story of the job in the distant town, they
would not have got so much money from me. If a
borrower tries to borrow money with no better
excuse than that he is penniless, it is our instinct to
put him off with five shillings or half-a-crown. A
man, we feel, cannot in decency expect a perfect
stranger to give him a pound or anything substantial
merely because he is starving. On the other hand,
if he can persuade us that he has just been appointed
assistant manager of the "Orkney and Shetland
Tailors' and Cutters' Standard," and that, if he does
not set off by the next train, he will lose the job, he
can with reasonable confidence ask for a sum large
enough to pay not only for his railway-ticket, but
for his meals on the train. And, if he approaches

the young and innocent, he will get it.  Thus we positively encourage borrowers to be dishonest.  We are likely to give more to a borrower who tells us a lie than to a borrower who tells us the truth.  I do not know how guileless youth can be protected against the machinations of people who want money for railway-fares.  The only thing to do is to let them learn by experience that most people who borrow money from strangers are frauds.  On the other hand, I know a man who, on finding himself without a penny in his pocket at Charing Cross, and yet under the necessity of getting to Hampstead within twenty minutes, went up to the first policeman he saw and asked him for the loan of his tube-fare.  And the policeman gave it to him.  That, I think, is one of the noblest incidents in the history of the London police force.  It should also be counted to the credit of the borrower that he paid the money back.

Few money-lenders, unfortunately, lend their money in the spirit of the policeman.  It is in vain that you will go into a money-lender's office and tell a specious story about your being in want of the fare to Hampstead or to Hawick.  The money-lender is not really interested in your needs, but in your possessions.  In order to get at his money you must appeal not to his heart but to his greed of gain.  I should not mind his doing this if he took any risks in his business.  But he will not lend you money if he thinks there is any risk in it.  He will not lend you a pound unless he is sure that, if you do not pay him back, he will get not only his pound, but considerably more. Do not be misled by his offers of £50,000 on your note of hand. I am not sure what a note of hand is, but the only money-lender whom I ever took at his word assured me that it meant my furniture. I will say this for him, that I never saw a more attractive advertisement. It had an air of generosity, of devil-may-care philanthropy, that went straight to my heart. I was myself young and generous at the time, and, deciding that it would be unfair to shear so obvious a lamb, I wrote to him, asking not for £50,000, but for £50. Frankly, I thought my letter was a note of hand, and I looked forward to receiving a cheque by return of post. But, instead of this, a man whom I thought, and whom most people would think, an odious little wretch, called at my flat, and made such outrageous proposals that I got rid of him as quickly as possible. It was quite clear that he was thinking, not of how much I wanted, but of how much he could get out of me. So far as I could see, money-lending was a mere business with him, and he had no intention of parting with a penny, unless he could be sure either of his right to seize all I had or of coming down for his money on some of my dearest friends. I was so astounded by his change of front that I had not the heart even to remind him of the terms of his advertisement. His face was simply an ill-shaven sneer. He was the sort of man whom you would not have asked for a crust of bread if you were starving. To tell the truth he not only destroyed my faith in money-lenders but he very nearly destroyed my faith in human nature.

The only other dealings I ever had with money-lenders occurred about the same time and they also were of a kind rather disturbing to the rosy optimism of youth. A poor woman called on me one day and reminded me that I had once known one of her second cousins. Having established this sentimental link between us she told me that she had been behaving rather foolishly and in order to pay her debts, had had to borrow £20. She asked me if I would mind signing a bill for it as a matter of form. I assured her that I hadn't £20 in the world. "It doesn't matter," she told me. "It's only a question of writing your signature. You'll never hear of it again." I accordingly put on my hat and went out with her to a money-lender's, where we both wrote our signatures, and she got the £20.

Everything went swimmingly for the first three or four weeks. I had an enthusiastic letter from her, in which she told me that she was paying off the debt in instalments and offered me a four-leaved shamrock. I wrote back, still more enthusiastically, for I was deeply moved by the offer of the four-leaved shamrock, but I said that I couldn't dream of taking such a precious mascot from her. She replied ecstatically, saying that she was still paying the instalments and that, if at any time she failed to do so, I was at liberty to tell her second cousin. I wrote back, almost on the verge of tears, assuring her that I had the utmost confidence in her, and

telling her that I wouldn't dream of saying anything
about the matter to her second cousin. A month
later I had a letter from the money-lender, saying
that the lady whose bill I had backed had fallen into
arrears with her payments and asking me what I
thought of doing about it. I wrote urging him to
write to her. I even wrote to her myself, expressing the hope that she was well, and explaining that
the money-lender seemed to be getting anxious about
his money. Some days later the letter came back
marked "Not known." I wrote again to the address
that she had given me, and learned that she had
gone away, leaving no address. Meanwhile the
money-lender kept sending me letters and calling
round on me, and, indeed, harassing me to such an
extent that in the end I saw I should have no peace
till I paid the money myself. In the result, I borrowed three weeks' salary in advance from the office
in which I worked and went round to the money-
lender and bought back my signature. It was the
highest price, I might say, that has ever been paid
for anything I have written. Mr. Arnold Bennett,
I believe, gets something between a shilling and a
guinea a word. But those two words that I wrote
were, even in the illiterate eyes of a money-lender,
reckoned to be worth between six and seven pounds
each.

In spite of my experiences, however, I am not in
entire sympathy with Lord Carson's campaign
against money-lenders. At least, I dislike some of
the arguments that are being used against them.

Some people seem to want to suppress money-lenders merely because they send them circulars through the post. I have seen a man raging when, on opening what looked like an interesting letter, he found that it was only a note from somebody in Bond Street, offering to lend him £50,000. I admit that, after one has passed the first flush of youth, it is a dullish sort of letter to receive, but I had much rather find a money-lender's circular in an envelope than a bill. If you want to purify the post, you should begin by prohibiting the transmission of bills. Money-lenders' circulars have the one shining merit that they are almost the only sort of letters that there is no need to answer. Apart from this, I am not sure that it is wise to discourage such model members of the community as the majority of money-lenders are. What other profession can show the same immunity from crime? Rarely do you hear of a money-lender committing murder. I do not think any respectable money-lender has ever been convicted of burglary. I doubt even if money-lenders run off with other people's wives as often as other people do. Most of them devote themselves quietly to their business, and are careful never to injure a fellow-creature except for purposes of gain and within the four corners of the law. I see that Lord Haldane was courageous enough to say in the House of Lords that "the money-lender is not always the ruffianly person he is supposed to be." That is a tribute of a kind of which any profession might well be proud. Has Lord Haldane ever paid a similar tribute to the clergy or to the medical or legal professions?

The money-lender, indeed, is a perfectly harmless person if you do not do business with him. And no one but a fool would do business with him. The wise man, if he finds that his debts are beyond his means, will go into the bankruptcy court or to jail or to South America rather than into the office of a money-lender. He knows that, if he cannot afford to pay his debts, he can afford much less to borrow the necessary money from a money-lender. One cannot pay one's debts by doubling them except, perhaps, in fairyland. No one, indeed, but a millionaire can afford to borrow money from a money-lender. And in the end I should back the money-lender to beat the millionaire. The money-lender combines the genius of a bull-dog with that of a boa-constrictor. He is one of the most fascinating of the lower animals.

## The Stranger's Room

THERE are words and phrases to which I never get accustomed, but which I use merely because they are the words and phrases that most other people seem to use. One of these words for a long time was "hassock." I had never known the word "hassock" outside a book till I left school; "boss" was the name by which I knew that enviable extra of the pew and the drawing-room. Legends had come down from an earlier generation concerning a struggle for a boss in a clergyman's pew one Sunday morning between two of the clergyman's children. ("Clergyman" is another word I dislike, though I like it better than "minister," which in that part of the world was more interchangeable with it than it is in England.) The clergyman had paused in his sermon to watch the tussle in the pew between his son and daughter, and then in a voice as from Sinai had ordered the little boy out of the church. Listening to the story, I could almost hear James's small shoes squeaking as with lowered head he passed down the aisle through the still and silent banks of the congregation. I became little James myself for the moment in my imagination, and, feeling his disgrace in every nerve, I could not believe that his father had been right to punish so severely so small a wrong. How stern the world seemed to have been from the expulsion out of Eden till shortly before the date of my own birth.

A word that I like as little as I like "hassock" is "spare-room." I found myself using it the other day, but instinctively I should have written not "the spare-room," but "the stranger's room." This was the name by which the best bedroom in the house was known to me as a child, and I cannot help thinking that it is a more charming name than the other. Idle the room might lie for days, for weeks, at a time, but it had a gleaming luxury of welcome, of invitation, for the stranger who would succeed the last stranger in the delightful procession. I had always liked strangers—at least, strangers who came on a visit to the house. Perhaps, I had begun early in life to associate them with food— with jellies and creams and with all kinds of dishes that were as beautiful as Mary Queen of Scots in their fantastic paper frills. A crowded house meant a crowded sideboard and a crowded table. Especially happy was the week in June during which the General Assembly sat and clergymen seemed to jump down in dozens from side-cars outside the gate one day after another. What preparations were made for them, with an extra cook brought in, and even the sexton, bearded and with shaven upper lip, impressed as a butler! What a paradise was the pantry for a hundred hours! To me at least it seemed as wonderful and as varied as if it had been brought into existence by a special act of creation. It was an oblong world worthy of violets and rose-leaves. Every separate jelly stood in a dish moulded into as noble a piece of architecture as the Parthenon. Here was a busy city of ratafias, whipped cream, sugared caraway-seeds, custards, jugs, bottles, pies, and a thousand delicacies to sharpen the palate of a child or a clergyman. It was on an occasion of this kind that a cook, with a taste for long words, finding me prying too closely among the shelves and the cupboards, cried fiercely: "Come away, Master Y., come away from them combustibles." Little did she know how impossible it was for me to stay away from the neighbourhood of whipped cream. I think there must be an element of the cat in me, for, at the sound of cream being whipped, I hastened in the direction of it as other people run to the scene of a fire. Was it only greed that was the cause of this early passion? Surely not, for I was happy to be allowed to sit with a bowl in my lap and whip the cream myself till my arm ached for no other reward than to be allowed to lick the fork at the end of my labours. The child who helps to whip cream or to beat up eggs with a patent egg-beater, is not a mere would-be guzzler, but is an assistant at a miracle. He is fascinated by the spectacle of a thing being turned into another kind of thing—of the commonplace being converted into the wonderful by human hands. As for the dinner itself, the table had to be lengthened, and two new leaves of mahogany let into it till it was almost as long as the room, and noble it looked surrounded by strangers from the ends of

the only earth in which one was interested. Had
they been the Knights of the Round Table, or the
Seven Champions of Christendom, or the Nine
Worthies of the World, my ears would not have
been wider open for their every word, as they sat,
each man with a thin glass of lemonade in which a
large block of ice floated at his right hand, and
taking part in a babel of conversation about giants
(who were Doctors of Divinity) and mighty wars
(which were fought on such issues as Home Rule,
and the right to sing hymns in the churches). You
who have never dined with Presbyterian ministers
as a child cannot be expected to know the savour
of the finest wit. I listen in vain nowadays for
those deft turnings of Scriptural phrase, those
anecdotes drawn from East of the Sun and West
of the Moon, that once rivalled the calves foot jelly
and the Bavarian cream as delights of the table.
It is impossible for anyone who has dined a great
deal with clergymen to go through life an atheist.
The clergyman in the pulpit may darken his mind
with doubt, but the clergyman at the table renews
his faith again.

It was not only at dinner, however, that there
were strangers in the house. There were strangers
at the breakfast-table, and the last sound one heard
at night before going to sleep was the sound of
strangers arriving at the door in cars. All day
long there was that sense of exhilaration—of pleasant grown-up men talking and laughing and smoking—of clergymen and clergymen's wives, of uncles,

second cousins, second cousins once removed, and whatnot. Each of them had come from a different part of the earth, and the ends of the earth seemed to have met in one small house. They were all from "the country," and, because of this, they seemed to me to be scarcely less wonderful than the horses and cows and hens among which they lived. That, I fancy, is the charm the stranger usually has for us. He comes from somewhere else. If he comes from the sea, he brings the sea with him into the room. If he comes from the farm, he brings a landscape with white-pillared gates and sloping fields and ruined stone walls and a ruined mill and animals at pasture. To sit in such company is to go on one's travels across happy rivers, along tree-bordered roads, and by the tumbling sea. The stranger is not only a man but a place—at least, he was in those days when his own name was scarcely better known to us than the name of the parish from which he came. And so, whether from their associations with food or from their associations with the country, I came to love strangers, and the house never seemed perfect until the stranger's room was occupied. A grandmother, an uncle, a cousin, someone unknown—I might have my preferences, but any stranger was better than no stranger at all. If, in my infant prayers, I used to petition for great wealth, it was chiefly in order that I might be able to build a house so large that it would be full of strangers' rooms, each of them occupied by a stranger from one year's

end to the other. To be exact, I had two houses
in my mind, one in the town and one in the country.
I could point out the sites, and, indeed, I have
them both still in my mind, but I have long since
lost hope. Nor did I intend to fill them merely
with people I knew—with the cousins and friends
I loved—but in dreams of so great wealth I foresaw
some of my heroes from the great world crossing the
sea as my guests. The best rooms of all were
occupied in these dreams by Mr. Joseph Chamberlain and his then youthful son, Austen. Those who
have never worshipped statesmen in their childhood can hardly imagine that mood of adoration
in which the name "Chamberlain" seemed to small
boys the most beautiful word in the English language. If I had been in a fever, and you had
mentioned the name "Chamberlain" to me I believe it would have calmed me. Once, indeed, when
I was in an agony of horror after something that
had been told me, an older cousin was able to re-
store me to calm only by describing a meeting at
which he had heard Joseph Chamberlain speaking
and his extraordinarily beautiful voice. I do not
know whether Chamberlain had a beautiful voice,
but it would have sounded beautiful to me. It is as
well, perhaps, that he never came to my house, for
I had theological as well as hospitable designs upon
him. I had a secret hope, indeed, of converting
both father and son to a belief in the Trinity. For,
devoted disciple that I was, I felt sad that their
prospects in the next world should be endangered

by their adhesion to Unitarianism. I had no doubt, however, that they had but to pay a few visits as my guests to a Presbyterian church to change all that. It was an unfair advantage to take of a visitor, but who would not save his hero's soul at all costs? In my dreams, Mr. Chamberlain was quite pleasant about the matter—nay, he was ultimately grateful.

Alas, as the world grows older, the houses become smaller, and it may be that the stranger's room will in another century have become a thing of the past. My friends, when they come to London, stay at hotels, and I do not even know whether I should like to see them at breakfast. I should be glad to know that they were having breakfast downstairs, but I doubt if after boyhood I had ever any genuine taste for nine-o'clock-in-the-morning hospitality except in a dream. Nor should I care to have my house overrun by strangers as by cats from year's end to year's end. I like strangers still, but within reason. If there were a stranger's room in the house, there are not above fifty people I should ever invite to occupy it, and not all of them might accept the invitation. In childhood the stranger was as a rule at once strange and intimate. In later life he is usually only strange. And who would be cooped up for more than a few hours at a time with people with whom he has no degree of intimacy? Hence, even if I had the wealth of an Eastern potentate, I doubt if to-day I should ever get further than dreaming about those two large houses warrened with stranger's rooms. But I like the name "The Stranger's Room" none the less on that account. It seems to me to recall a world in which time moved slowly and men were hospitable and the stranger entering the house was as welcome as an angel, and often proved to be an extremely amusing angel.

## On Being Measured for a Suit of Clothes

HOW gravely the words run into the rhythm of blank verse! Milton himself never wrote a line of blank verse that was more impeccable. Emotion, it is said, generates rhythm of speech, and who can enter a tailor's shop without emotion? I have certainly never been able to do so. And I am not sure that this is entirely due to the tailor. The truth is, I seldom call on him except when the only alternative is a quarrel and a lasting breach with my relations. First, there are weeks of mild admonition: "You ought to have some new clothes. You are getting quite shabby." Gradually the tone of command creeps in: "You must have new clothes. Do ask E. V. the name of his tailor." A week later italics make their appearance: "You *must* get a new suit." Italics quickly give way to small capitals: "YOU MUST get a NEW SUIT. Will you go and get measured this afternoon?" "No, no," I protest, "to-day is Friday. Nothing would persuade me to be measured for a new suit on a Friday." "Well, then, on Monday." Luckily, Monday is usually the thirteenth or something equally impossible, and I have another good argument for postponement. A few days later there is an appeal to my better nature in the form of an outrageous falsehood: "You know you promised." This fails, as it deserves

to fail, but at last there comes a morning when I
find myself in a corner, threatened with both horns
of a dilemma: "Will you go and get measured to-
day, or shall I call for you in town and take you?"
It is tyranny, but I know that I am beaten: "All
right, but he's sure to want a deposit, and I haven't
any money." "Give him a cheque." "If I'm so
shabby as you say I am, he'd probably refuse it."
"Well, call in at the butcher's and get him to cash a
cheque on your way into town." "I don't know
the butcher." "That doesn't matter. He probably knows you. He must often have seen you
passing." "If I'm so shabby as you say I am, he
probably took me for a tramp." "Now you see
what comes of dressing so badly. You're frightened of your own butcher." "No, I'm not. I'm
frightened of bringing disgrace on all of you by
being arrested in a butcher's shop for trying to
get money by false pretences." "Oh, well, I'll come
with you as far as the butcher's." "Don't trouble,
I'll cash a cheque in town myself. But really I don't
know when I'll have time to go to the tailor's. I
promised to lunch with Jones to-day." "I'll ring
up Mr. Jones and explain." "Oh, don't trouble.
Besides, I'm not sure that he didn't say yesterday
that he wouldn't be able to come." Certainly a man
would need to be an eel in order to be able to
argue with a woman. Women have such a talent
for shifting their ground that one has at times to
resort to positive invention in order to keep up
with them. "Good-bye," I say sullenly, as I put

on my coat, for I hate having my day ruined like this; "what did you say the tailor's name was?" "I think it was Turtle, or Tompkinson, or Tarbutt, or some name like that. Anyhow, you'll be able to find him quite easily. He's Alan's tailor." "What's his number?" I ask gloomily, for I know at least the name of the street. "I don't know his number, but Alan said his shop was at the wrong end of the street." "Which is the wrong end of the street?" "I don't know. Go and look at it and see." "But in what way is it the wrong end? Is it wrong morally, or architecturally, or socially? Does he mean that it's the dear end or the cheap end?" "Oh, the cheap, I'm sure." "Honestly, I think I ought to put off going till we've seen Alan again and got some information about his tailor."

Excellent though my reasoning was, I found myself later in the day walking along a street which seemed to be mainly inhabited by tailors, and turning over in my mind the problem of how to find the right shop in the wrong end of it. I walked up and down it twice till an idle policeman began to look at me. I felt that I must dive before long into some shop or other if only in order to escape his scrutiny. The nearest approach to Turtle or Tompkinson or Tarbutt that I saw among the names on the shops was Pigeon, so I opened the door and went in. "I want to be measured for a suit," I said. "Thank you, sir," he said; "what colour?" I said dark grey, for I had been told to say dark grey. As he looked among the rolls of cloth, he

asked, "Any recommendation?" "Mr. Hereward
gave me your name," I said. "We always like," he
said, "to know the name of anyone who sends us
a new customer so that we may write and thank
him." I had a curious feeling of elation at that.
Here was I who had been called disgracefully
shabby, and had been talked to as if I were a scare-
crow or an old rag-and-bone man, and yet a respectable tailor was about to write and thank a
man of fashion for having introduced me to him.
"Either," I thought, "I cannot be so shabby-looking
after all, or the tailor sees that beneath a shabby
waistcoat there possibly beats a purse of gold."

I warmed to the tailor to such a degree in consequence that, when he unrolled a length of dark grey
cloth, I said. "Yes, that will do excellently." He
said, "There's another cloth I'd like to show you,"
and he showed it to me. I looked at it, and said:
"I think I'll have that one." "But," he declared,
"if you prefer something darker, here's something
that might suit you," and spread a third cloth on the
top of the other two. "Yes," I said, looking at
it, "I think that's the nicest of the three." "But,"
said the tailor, producing yet another roll of cloth,
"if you want something that will last for ever, I
have a pattern here that I think will please you."
"Yes," I agreed, "I like that very much. I think
I'll have that." "But," cried the tailor, "if you
think you'd like something else better—" "No,
no," I pleaded, "don't show me any more. It only
makes it more difficult to choose." "Well," he

agreed, "I don't think you'll be disappointed in any of those that I have shown you. Which did you say you preferred?" I took up one of the cloths between my finger and thumb, and said with an air of decision, "That one." "Oh," he said, tugging one of the others into view, "you would rather have it than this one?" I looked at this one, hesitated and was lost. "No," I said, "I think I'll have this one." "Of course," he said, watching my face closely and then pointing at the third of the cloths, "you'll not get the same wear out of any of them as out of that." I nodded consideringly. "Well, perhaps, after all," I said, "I'd better have that." As to which of the cloths I chose in the end, I know no more than Adam. It was an exhausted frame that the tailor led off into an inner room to undergo the ordeal of tape measurement.

I stood in the midst of a superfluity of mirrors while he measured me as unemotionally as if I had been a corpse. As he measured, he and an invisible man outside the door kept talking in the strange jargon of numbers that nobody but a tailor can understand. "41½," called the tailor loudly. "41½," came the far-away answer of the ghost. "18½," declared the tailor *forte*. "18½," repeated the ghost *piano*. "12¾," lustily insisted the tailor. "12¾," weakly wailed the ghost. "By the way," I interrupted this extraordinary conversation after a time, "I suppose you have noticed that I carry a good many things in my pockets. I hope you won't have the clothes too well cut, for

I should only spoil them." "I see what you mean,"
said the tailor, "you would like them a little loose."
"Loose," I assented, "but not too loose." "I see,"
said he, "and the trousers?" "Oh, just ordinary
trousers." "Ordinary trousers," he called out to
the ghost. "Trousers ordinary," piped the ghost.
Noting a certain disappointment in his voice, I asked
him: "What is the opposite of ordinary in trousers?
Do you mean turned-up or do you mean the sort of
trousers 'Punch' makes fun of?" "Well, trousers
are being worn a little wider this year. I think
wider trousers would suit you." "Well," said I,
looking in the glass, and catching a glimpse of a
pair of legs in ordinary trousers, "if you think so,
I don't mind having them a little wider, so long
as you don't make them as wide as the trousers in
'Punch.'" "Oh, no," he said; "the great art in
dress, as in everything else, is not to run to ex-
tremes." I rather suspect that the origin of the
Oxford trousers was the mistake of a tailor who
got his numbers mixed and put the waist-measure-
ment in the wrong place. The tailor told me that
he had recently cut a pair of trousers for an under-
graduate which measured forty-four inches round
the foot. I have no head for figures, but I think
he said forty-four. Having pledged him to attempt
no extravagance of this kind on me, I permitted
him to aim at a decorous compromise. This, I
fancy, pleased him, for when, as I was coming away,
I offered to pay him some money in advance, he
brushed the offer aside lightly. "Oh, no," he said,

"we don't require anything of that kind from anyone with a good recommendation." As I came
out of the door, I looked up and down the wrong
end of the street and asked myself: "Can this be
London or am I in Heaven?"

Since then, I have been back to have the suit
"tried on" for the first time. It did not, perhaps,
look at its best as the tailor covered it with chalk-
marks and ripped away a temporary canvas collar.
"How do you like the sleeves?" he asked me. "I
think they're exactly right," I said. "Just a shade
on the long side?" he suggested. "Well," I agreed,
"perhaps just a shade." And he took a piece of
chalk and drew a line round the cuff, assuring me
that they would look much better half an inch
shorter. "And the waistcoat—does the opening
come down far enough?" "Yes, I think it's just
right." "Perhaps, just another inch or so?"
"Well, perhaps." "And the coat—is it quite long
enough?" And he turned a mirror so that it reflected another mirror which in turn reflected my
back. It was, I confess, a view to humiliate even
a proud man. Impossible to describe it as the back
of a Greek god or to pretend that it was as straight
as an arrow. Then the bald patch at the back of
the head—the last time I had seen it was at a tailor's
when it was no larger than a baby's palm. Since
then it had spread till it was now a very pool of
atrichia. "God knows," thought I, as I surveyed
the back of the strange figure in the glass within the
glass, "for such as you any old suit would serve.

You and your new clothes," I reflected bitterly. "Go back to your shabbiness. You are mortal, and the very crown of your head bears evidences of your decay." I came out into the street, pondering on the brevity of human life.

I walked slowly till I came to the right end of the street. Then, as I turned the corner, I suddenly remembered something. "I must get a new hat," I said.

## The Latchkey

I HAVE been reading some letters from fathers and mothers in a newspaper correspondence on the subject of latchkeys. I gather from this that a latchkey is a symbol of liberty. I myself have had a latchkey for more than half my life, but I have long since ceased to feel liberated on that account. No doubt, I should notice the absence of the latchkey, but I do not notice its presence, and am no more grateful for it than for the fact that I am not in jail. If I were in jail—and, if I am not, let it be put down to good fortune rather than to merit—I am sure I should be longing for freedom, and by freedom I should mean being out of jail. I should envy everybody who was not in jail as a lord of liberty, and should think that the air he breathed was better than wine and that his very step must reveal his delight in his freedom. Being out of jail, however, I cannot picture myself as a man to be envied. The experience of not being in jail seems to me a very commonplace experience and nothing, as people say, to shout about. I know many other men who are not in jail. Some of them are so melancholy that you would conclude that not being in jail must be a tragic fate. I fancy, indeed, that they would be far happier if they were

sent to jail for a week every year, for they might
then realize during the rest of the year their comparative, if not superlative, luck in being out of it.
It is the same with latchkeys. Many of the people
who possess latchkeys are as miserable as if all the
woes of the world had befallen them. Disappointed
ambition, lost love, fear of illness, fear of poverty,
bad conscience, cunning suspicion—what can a latchkey do to soothe or to heal the victims of these
widespread ills? No weeping philosopher has ever
counted the absence of a latchkey among the great
troubles of life, and no laughing philosopher has
ever counted the possession of a latchkey among the
supreme joys, or has praised life on the ground that
latchkeys had made it not only endurable but
glorious. You might infer from this that a latchkey is a trivial thing. But you would be wrong.
Let even the broken-hearted lover be denied a latchkey by his landlady and told that he must be in the
house by ten and he will rage as if fate had begun
a new persecution of him. He will almost forget his
broken heart as he escapes from the house at the
earliest possible moment as from a prison. There
are small country hotels in which visitors are told
that the doors will be locked at half-past ten and
no latchkeys are provided; I should fret against
even so temporary a restriction of my liberty. If,
by some inconceivable accident, I were suddenly forbidden to use a latchkey at home, I should feel that
I was the most deeply-wronged man on earth, and,
forgetting that the world is suffering still worse

than I, either from growing pains or from the pangs of dissolution—I am not sure which—I should concentrate all my energies on getting the prohibition ended. In my imagination every latchkey would be a golden key, an end in itself, a piece of treasure. I should see the human race divided into men who had latchkeys and men who had none, and I should think of those who had none as helots.

That is the sort of paradox in which we are usually landed. We should be unhappy if we had no latchkeys, but we are not any happier for having them. The only happiness we obtain through having them is the happiness of escaping the unhappiness of not having them. I am not any happier for knowing that I may stay out till three or four in the morning. I do not wish to stay out till three or four in the morning, and as a rule, indeed, am tired of life about two. My latchkey offers me these liberties, and I quietly refuse them. I doubt, indeed, if a latchkey is worth having except to those who ought not to be allowed to have them. Some of the parents who are writing to the Press on the subject praise the latchkey eloquently because, if you give latchkeys to the young, it shows that you trust them. But I do not trust the young in this general fashion. What have the young in the mass ever done since the beginning of the world that we should trust them? It was our first parents who committed the first sin, but it was the younger generation who committed the first murder. I do not

pretend that the young are not as virtuous as ourselves, but they have not yet been frightened into
a kind of common sense so that I do not see any
reason for a blind confidence in them. We of an
older generation can scarcely trust ourselves; we
certainly cannot trust each other—otherwise, why
all these policemen, crossed-cheque systems and wit-
nessed contracts?—how, then, should we trust a
race of which we know so little as we do of our
juniors? I do not deny that there is a large proportion of trustworthy human beings in every generation—that some, like Casabianca, are born trustworthy and that still more have trustworthiness
thrust on them by circumstances. But a generaliza-
tion that would say that all human beings, or nearly
all, were to be trusted, would be utterly ridiculous
and a denial of experience. Yet we can scarcely
help making foolish generalizations of this kind,
and even living by them. At one period we are for
trusting everybody; at another, we are for trusting
nobody. We swing between the passion for liberty
—which is the period of trust—and the passion
for law and order—which is the period of distrust.
Liberty, like a latchkey, is most beautiful when we
do not possess it. And so is law and order. No
country has ever yet discovered the perfect compromise between the two, which would give men
liberty and order in permanently just proportions.
A fight for liberty usually ends in the establishment
of a dictatorship by those who have fought for
liberty. The moment at which law and order is

supreme is frequently the moment at which it is in greatest danger from the rising passion for liberty. The truth is that neither liberty nor law and order works. The truth is that nothing works. We creep along somehow or other, changing our theories as women change their fashions in clothes. We feel that anything is better than last year's clothes. We feel that anything is better than the theory of the last generation.

During the nineteenth century, many people thought that the British Constitution was a perfect compromise between liberty and law and order, and it seemed to them to work so well that, if human beings were wise, it would last for ever. But conceptions of liberty have changed, and young men and maidens would now laugh derisively if you spoke of the British Constitution of Tennyson's day as being, as he said of the throne, "broad-based upon the people's will." Certainly, a great many people were poor and a great many people were miserable under the British Constitution when it seemed most praiseworthy, and men have since then been struggling, not only for more political liberty, but for more economic and moral liberty—for liberty, indeed, such as would have seemed to Tennyson the wildest anarchy. They have achieved many of these liberties, but they are not yet free. They will probably be tired of liberty long before they are free. For there are always enough people who abuse liberty at a fairly early stage to disgust or intimidate the rest into a reaction against it. Then returns the love of order in politics, morals and the arts. Man ceases to be regarded as an angel to be trusted and is looked on as a private soldier to be subjected to authority.

Perhaps it is the genius of the English that, more than any other race, they have achieved a compromise that prevents both the more disgusting kinds of abuse of liberty and the more disgusting kinds of abuse of law and order. In politics and in morals they have trusted human nature, but not too far. They have distrusted human nature but not unreasonably. They have never idealized liberty as the French at times have, and they have never idealized law and order except for the purpose of holding down some subject people. Hence there is at most times enough liberty in England to make revolution unlikely, and enough law and order to make Fascism seem undesirable even to the naturally Conservative. All men aspire after liberty, but the Englishman, while loving it as well as anybody, knows that there is not nearly as much in it as the enthusiasts suppose.

He is, I fancy, a mystic in his attitude to liberty beyond the inhabitants of most countries. The excessive worship of liberty is usually a materialistic passion. It is founded on a belief that man is the prisoner of external forces, and that, if he were released from them, it would be into a heaven upon earth. The Englishman acts on the assumption that there is no key in politics or anywhere outside himself that can open the door into such a paradise.

If he opens the door to the prisoner, he does not promise him that there are ambrosia and nectar awaiting him outside. It is a curious paradox that a race that has done so much for political liberty and that insists beyond any other race on having it should have so little theoretic passion for it. But the lack of this passion is justified by experience. Liberty is not a way of working out men's destinies for them, but a way of enabling them to work out their own destinies. Escaped out of prison, man is still a prisoner to himself. Hence his too frequent melancholy air when he finds himself in possession of every conceivable liberty from external circumstances—rich, uncontrolled, above criticism, a free citizen of a free nation. If he is not the prisoner of his habits, he is the prisoner of his impulses. If he is not the prisoner of his principles, he is the prisoner of his desires. It seems absurd for such a helpless creature to perturb himself about the possession of a latchkey. Rather you would expect to find him looking about for the key that would admit him into the perfect prison. And perhaps that is what most men do.

Poets seek the confinement of metre and form. Religious men shackle themselves with a creed. Moralists lock themselves in with the iron key of principle. Politicians are unhappy till they have made themselves slaves to a party. It is one of the chief aims of life, I fancy, to escape from compulsory imprisonment and then, as soon as possible, to submit ourselves to voluntary imprisonment. We must assume the chains ourselves, or Nature will rivet them on us in spite of ourselves. Meanwhile, let us have latchkeys, by all means. But they don't really matter a brass farthing.

## Silence

SILENCE is unnatural to man. He begins life with a cry and ends it in stillness. In the interval he does all he can to make a noise in the world, and there are few things of which he stands in more fear than of the absence of noise. Even his conversation is in great measure a desperate attempt to prevent a dreadful silence. If he is introduced to a fellow mortal, and a number of pauses occur in the conversation, he regards himself as a failure, a worthless person, and is full of envy of the emptiest-headed chatterbox. He knows that 99 per cent. of human conversation means no more than the buzzing of a fly, but he longs to join in the buzz and to prove that he is a man and not a wax-work figure. The object of conversation is, not for the most part, to communicate ideas; it is to keep up the buzzing sound. There are, it must be admitted, different qualities of buzz; there is even a buzz that is as exasperating as the continuous ping of a mosquito. But at a dinner-party one would rather be a mosquito than a mute. Most buzzing, fortunately, is agreeable to the ear, and some of it is agreeable even to the mind. He would be a foolish man, however, who waited until he had a wise thought to take part in the buzzing with his neighbours. Those who despise the weather as a conversational opening seem to me to be ignorant of the reason why human beings wish to talk. Very few human beings join in a conversation in the hope of learning anything new. Some of them are content if they are merely allowed to go on making a noise into other people's ears, though they have nothing to tell them except that they have seen two or three new plays or that they had bad food in a Swiss hotel. At the end of an evening during which they have said nothing at immense length, they justly plume themselves on their success as conversationalists. I have heard a young man holding up the monologue of a prince among modern wits for half an hour in order to tell us absolutely nothing about himself with opulent long-windedness. None of us except the young man himself liked it, but he looked as happy as if he had had a crown on his head.

Many of us, indeed, do not enjoy conversation unless it is we ourselves who are making the most conspicuous noise. This, I think, is a vice in conversation, but it has its origin in a natural hatred of silence. The young man was so much afraid of silence that he dared not risk being silent himself lest a universal silence should follow. If he failed as a talker, it was because he did not sufficiently realize that conversation should be not only a buzz but a sympathetic buzz. That is why the weather is so useful a subject. It brings people at once to an experience which is generally shared and enables them, as it were, to buzz on the same note. Having

achieved this harmony, they advance by miraculous
stages to other sympathies, and, as note succeeds
note, a pleasant and varied little melody of conversation is made, as satisfying to the ear and mind
as the music of a humming-top. The discovery of
new notes of sympathy is the secret of all good conversation. It is because this is necessary to good
conversation that a conversation of a party of three
is so often a failure. Two of them discover a note
of sympathy and they begin to buzz on it enthusiastically, forgetful of the fact that it is an occasion not for a double but for a triple buzz. Two of
them, perhaps, have been at the same college of the
same university. They go on for an hour happily
sharing experiences in sentences like "You remember old Crocker?" "You remember the day he—?"
"You remember the night he stole the policeman's
helmet?" "But the funniest thing of all was the
day he threw the bowl of tulips out of the window
and nearly brained old —" (naming a famous pro-
fessor of Greek). Reminiscences are the best conversation in the world for two; they warm the heart
and excite the brain like wine. But the third man
is all the more conscious of being out in the cold,
because these names and events, which are a sort
of algebraic symbols of the emotions to them, are
to him meaningless. He does not know who "old
Towser" was, or "old Billy Tubbs," or "old Snorter
Richardson." He smiles mechanically as the others
laugh with dreamier and dreamier eyes over incidents that convey all the fun of youth to them but

that to him seem mere inanities of the memory.
A conversation of this kind is bad, indeed, because
it condemns the third man to the torture of compulsory silence. You may have an excellent conversation of three where one man is voluntarily
silent, but you cannot have good conversation where
one of the three is necessarily silent.

It is not only in our social life, however, that we
dread silence. We love noise more than we know,
even when no other human being is present. When
we go from town to live in the country we deceive
ourselves if we think we are doing so in order to
exchange noise for quietness. We go into the country, not in order to escape from noise, but in search
of a different kind of noise. Sit in a country garden
in May and you will notice that the noise is continuous. The birds are as loquacious as women: the
bees as inimical to silence as children. Cocks crow,
hens cackle, dogs bark, sheep baa, cartwheels crunch,
and the whole day passes in a succession of sounds
which would drive us to distraction if we were
really devotees of silence. When evening falls, and
the voice of the last cuckoo fades into a universal
stillness, we are aware of a new awe as of something
supernatural. The fear of the dark is largely a fear
of silence. It is difficult to believe that the world is
entirely uninhabited, and, if it is not filled with the
noises of men and animals, we begin—at least, a
good many of us do—to suspect the silent presence
of something unseen and terrible. Noise is com-
panionship, and I remember that I, as a child, liked

even the ticking of a clock in the bedroom. How good it was, too, to open the bedroom window and hear the pleasant prose of a corn-crake coming from the meadows through the darkness! There are sounds that are terrifying at night, but they are chiefly so because of the stillness that is broken by them. The breathing of a cow behind a hedge, as you pass along a silent road at midnight, may startle you, but it is not the cow, it is the silence, that has startled you. If Nature, indeed, could contrive to maintain all her busy sounds through the night, darkness would lose more than half its terrors.

For complete silence produces feelings of awe in us even in the full blaze of day. If you could imagine yourself the last living thing on earth but the plants, and if you knew that you were immortal and secure from danger for ever, what horror you would feel of a world in which there was no sound but the sound of your own feet or of your own voice if you had the heart to use it! If there were birds and dogs and cats and cows and sheep, you might endure your solitude with philosophy. I should not care for it myself even then, but I should suffer less than if I were the last living creature on a silent globe, on which a motionless sea never broke the stillness on any shore. We speak of the silence of the grave, and without noise the world would be no better than a grave. To survive alone upon its lifeless surface would be to be buried alive, and most of us, if we were given the choice, would commit suicide in order to escape from it. This is not to say that we never enjoy the awfulness of silence. Travellers in the mountains and among the snows, discoverers of dead and deserted cities, can thrill us with their descriptions of the profound stillness of the scenes, as though to penetrate into such silence were to step into a new world. Silence such as this keys us up to unaccustomed excitements and susceptibilities. London seen from Westminster bridge in the silence of dawn moved Wordsworth with a majesty unknown in the busy clamour of noon. In silence we seem to approach the border of some mysterious reality that has escaped us in the din of common life. Hence it is that, if we go into a cathedral, we are offended by those who bring into it noise and restlessness. The cathedral moves us most deeply in perfect stillness. It is no mere superstition that bids us be silent or, if we must speak, lower our voices to a whisper. We cannot even see the cathedral so that its beauty passes into the imagination and the memory save in perfect silence.

Certain religious bodies have recognized the value of silence, and mystics have told us that it is through silence rather than through speech that we arrive at a knowledge of the secret of life. Certainly the increase in the noisiness of mankind does not seem to lead to any great increase of wisdom. Cynics are doubtful whether any useful end is served by the ceremony of the Two Minutes' Silence that has now become an annual event in England and some other countries on Armistice Day; but having been in a London street when all the traffic died down into perfect stillness, and every human being in sight stood motionless as a stone in a silent world, I, like a million others have felt the spell of the transformation. London of the bus and dray and warehouse seemed to be touched with a mystery and strangeness that meant more to the imagination than the hooting of horns and the hurry of trampling feet. One aged man, indeed, did advance through the deathlike stillness of the figures of his fellow creatures—an aged man in a faded bowler and with a pipe in his mouth. I do not know whether he even noticed that men and women had suddenly become statues and that the traffic of the streets was as still as the palace of the Sleeping Beauty. There was no sound on earth for a time but the whisper and squeaking of the old man's boots becoming less and less as it disappeared into the distance. Instead of breaking the silence, it seemed to intensify it. And no one even turned a head to look after him. Perhaps, he had never heard of Armistice Day. Perhaps—lucky man—he had never heard even of the War. But how typical he was of his kind in his incapacity for remaining still! The rest of us, it is true, can succeed in remaining silent for two minutes. But, at the sound of the gun, with what a cheerful tumult we rush back again into the clamour of ordinary life!

## First Class

THERE are worse places for spending a holiday —at least, for spending an Easter holiday— than bed. You do not congratulate yourself, perhaps, as you lie unable to read, unwilling to talk or even to be talked to, with an aching head, aching eyes, and little shivers of seedling aches in your legs, when the thermometer in your mouth is a burden and the doctor is sent for because it has risen above 103°—a temperature peculiarly detestable because, while it has all the dullness of mediocrity, it is high enough to destroy the pleasures of placidity. But when the doctor has called, and you have taken the first dose of the bottle of febrifuge, and have begun to dissolve into a Christian again, little by little the world returns to your senses and, with a dose from the bottle every four hours even during a sleepless night, you find yourself taking pleasure in the acclamation of the blackbirds and the very sparrows at sunrise, and with an interest in the doings of your fellow-creatures that makes a newspaper last you four or five times as long as it does when you are well. How wonderful the Wembley Exhibition seems, if you read about it in bed! I do not mean to cast a doubt upon its wonders in reality, and I am sure I shall find myself wandering by its quiet lake, and travelling on its railway that never stops, and pausing with marvelling eyes to watch the wheels of machines going round, and staring at palaces that (unlike some royal palaces) look really like palaces, and getting lost in African swamps and British Guiana, and enjoying the lighter side of life provided by Wembley Amusements, Ltd., and, after an hour or two of it all, sitting down under the flag of J. Lyons and Co. to a pot of China tea, and wondering whether this, on the whole, is not the best feature of the Exhibition—I shall do this, no doubt, like every other mortal who has the chance, and I shall count myself happy. But I doubt if I shall ever get the same impression of Wembley with the eye that I can get so easily by reading the papers in a sick bed. The place begins to seem to me a sort of earthly paradise, one of the world's wonders, greater than Babylon and its hanging gardens, a blaze of glory that must be visible to the inhabitants of Mars, a rival of Rome the deathless. Upon my word, I got the impression from reading one paper that the opening of the Wembley Exhibition was an event of such world-wide significance that (though this was Easter Week) the Resurrection was a trifle to it. Were I to go on lying in bed, how Prospero's wand would come to my aid and set this recurrent fabric of a vision before my eyes! How I should long to be able to get up and go and see it, and how much more I should really enjoy it because I had not seen it but only imagined it!

How delightful even a Bank Holiday seems if one is lying in bed! How charming the sunshine that

streams through the windows! How sweet the blue
sky and the voices of the birds! The hedge sparrow
in the garden, whose winter song has been so shy
and timid, is now singing as if he were challenging
any of the birds newly come from Africa to match
him. None of the migrants has yet appeared in this
suburb and in thei. absence his challenge grows daily
bolder. Nor, indeed, does one require these foreign
·irds in order to be reasonably happy. Already
on a morning or evening of sunshine there is enough
din in the gardens without the addition of clamorous
aliens. There is, indeed, one starling that itself
makes more noise than a heath of nightingales. It
seems to go from garden to garden screeching in its
own language. "Help! Help! Murder! Murder!" At first when you hear it from a neighbouring garden you imagine that it has got caught in a
net or been seized by a cat or that somebody is
robbing its nest; but you find that it goes round all
the gardens in the road along with the other star-
lings screeching, "Help! Help! Murder! Murder!" from the trees in exactly the same way. We
know it now as The Mad Starling. I have not seen
it; but these things are described to me by my niece,
who is so good at looking out of the window. She
keeps me in touch from hour to hour with the wild
life of the garden. "I say," she says, looking out,
"Freaky has just chased a blackbird away from a
piece of bread in the next garden." "Freaky" is
her name for a sparrow in these parts with a peculiar
disease of the scalp which has left him bald and

wicked-looking as a vulture. At first when we saw him he looked so extraordinary that we had great hopes that he was a bird of a kind that no one had ever seen before in this island. I, with my childish belief in miracles, began at once to dream of going down to history with Freaky's assistance with a modest but secure place among the ornithologists. My niece with a more realistic eye than mine, however, insisted from the first that the bird was only a bald sparrow. I was all the gladder to know that a blackbird had been deceived like myself by the evil face and the hunch of feathers behind the neck so that he had fled as from a bird of prey.

A few minutes later my niece had other wonders to report from the garden. "You know that piece of mutton fat hanging from the ash tree," she said; "—a blackbird has just jumped up at it from the ground and taken some in its beak and run away to eat it." "It didn't hang on to the fat upside-down like a tit?" I asked. "No," she replied, "it just jumped up at it. Wasn't it clever?" "Very," I agreed; "I didn't know blackbirds ate fat." "Neither did I," said my niece. So that in this respect we were happy in sharing the excitement of new discovery.

The tits themselves provide me with a constant interest. I cannot see them from my bed; but from time to time my niece at the window tells me, "There's a blue tit on the fat," or "There's a great tit in the rhododendrons, and I think it's looking at the monkey nuts on the table. Now it has hopped

on to the table and is eating the monkey nuts."
Still more exciting is the news when she tells me,
"The blue tits are back at the nesting-box again.
One of them has gone inside and the other is looking in at the hole." "Have they begun to build
yet?" I ask. "No," she says, "I left bits of cotton
wool all over the garden for them yesterday, to
make their nests with, but I think the sparrows
came and stole it all." It would be tedious to
give a detailed account of the world thus seen from
a bedroom window and through the eyes of another;
but I assure you if you were lying in bed you would
find it an extremely agreeable world, like a world
seen in a quiet dream. Your bed becomes a throne
of pleasure like the couch of an Epicurean deity and
gives you that sense of irresponsible remoteness
from the tumult of civilized men that is the easiest
means of cheerfulness. Civilized man in the meantime is riding on merry-go-rounds and blowing
whistles and eating whelks and ice-creams and
throwing hard balls at coconuts and buying balloons
for the children and throwing darts in order to win
a clock for his wife or a mouth organ for his eldest
son and doing his best to enjoy himself and to make
other people feel that they are enjoying themselves
amid noises from which the ear shrinks and smells
from which the nose shrinks and foods and liquors
from which the stomach shrinks. How I used to
enjoy it all myself when a crowd and the colour of
a showman's town seemed excitements enough to
make a day happy! But now, alas, I flee from such

pleasures and count myself happy to be shut off from
them within the four primrose-coloured walls of a
bedroom. I do not even hear, though the distance
is short enough, the voices of those desperate men
who try to persuade you to throw balls at coconuts.
I do not even hear the steam organs of the round-
abouts until the songs of the blackbirds have ceased
after sunset, when, the air having grown still, there
come stealing in at the north window, dim as a far
away chorus of angels, the strains of "Destiny,"
mingled with those of "Yes, We Have No
Bananas." At once the vast and raucous orgy of
the Bank Holiday comes before me as a scene of
torchlight and smoke-cloud, of tent and wooden
horse and painted tower, of trinkets and sweet-
meats, and of men and women and children moving
in the midst of it as bright and as smiling-cheeked
as marionettes.

But it was not of Bank Holidays that I sat down,
or rather sat up—for I am in bed at the moment—
to write. It was rather of the many thoughts that
flicker in incoherent procession through one's brain
as one lies ill in bed. Or, rather, it was of one of
that procession of thoughts that I halted on its
way as I was reading the day's papers. I do not
know why I should have been roused to such a
pitch of controversial pugnacity by reading attacks
in various papers on the first class railway passes
to be given to Members of Parliament. I have
no great wish to see Members of Parliament made
more comfortable than other men, and I think

that my indignation must have been stirred not on
behalf of Members of Parliament but on behalf
of first class railway travel. There has grown up
in these days an appalling and fallacious idea that
first class travel is a mere luxury, and that somehow or other it is not democratic. In point of fact,
first class travel is no more of a luxury than a first
class pair of boots. A man may spend his super-
fluous shillings on purchasing a first class rather
than a third class railway-ticket with as much democratic justification for his extravagance as when he
spends his money on English rather than on New
Zealand lamb. Everyone who has had to mix railway travel with work to a great extent knows that
it makes a considerable difference to him on many
occasions whether he has travelled first or third
class. By travelling first class he preserves energies
for his work which are otherwise frequently exhausted by breathing the foul air of an over-crowded
carriage, by keeping his legs out of the way of the
man's opposite, by trying to sit comfortably in a
space within which it is impossible to sit comfortably
for more than a few minutes. Hence I do not see
why we should grudge Members of Parliament a
comfortable seat on their travels to their constitu-
encies, any more than we grudge them the many
conveniences they enjoy in the House of Commons.
It would be possible for Members to assemble in a
third class House of Commons, in which the smok-
ing-room would have only straight-backed wooden
chairs, and in which the benches in the House itself

instead of being cushioned would be topped with the
cheapest slate.  Or they might even be compelled
to meet in Hyde Park, where they could sit on the
grass.  The truth is, certain comforts and conveniences are necessary to the efficiency of civilized
man, and both the Civil Service and the great business houses recognize this in their attitude to first
class railway travel.  The Labour ideal of railway
travel, I take it, is not an ideal of universal third
class railway travel, but of universal first class railway travel.  When I travel myself and have sufficient money in my pocket, this is the ideal I try to
live up to.  Hence from the charity of a sick bed I
am not going to blame a Member of Parliament for
doing what I myself do without shame and with a
better conscience than that with which I eat many a
luxurious dinner.

## Gratis

A CURIOUS incident is reported from Montreal. A local brewery announced that it would give a bottle of beer to anyone who applied for it on Friday evening, with the result that a crowd of twenty-five thousand collected and stormed the brewery doors. The police reserves had in the end to be called out to beat back a mob that included cripples, mothers holding babies, and (so the report says) "people of all walks in life." I fancy this is an exaggeration. There are several "walks in life" which, I am perfectly sure, were unrepresented in the attack on the brewery. I am confident, for example, that not a single bishop was present and very few clergymen. We can also take it for granted that doctors and lawyers were "conspicuous by their absence." It would be interesting, again, to inquire if the crowd contained a single industrial magnate or a single higher-division Civil Servant. Canada is, admittedly, a more democratic country than England, but it is difficult to believe that even in Canada there are not certain snobbish sections of society which would be too proud to take part in the storming of a brewery. Still, if the estimate of the size of the crowd is correct, about one in twenty of the inhabitants of Montreal was present —a figure which suggests either that the citizens are

exceedingly fond of beer or that they are exceedingly
fond of getting something for nothing. Would
there have been as big a crowd outside a mineral
water factory, I wonder, if bottles of ginger beer
had been given away gratis? The crowd might have
been as large, but I cannot help thinking that the
composition of the crowd would have been different.
There would have been fewer mothers and more
babies present. Children "of all walks in life"
would undoubtedly have turned up and fought round
the doors. But some grim and determined faces
would have been missing. These are thirsts that no
known mineral water can quench, and these, we may
be sure, were the inspiring soul of the crowd that
stormed the brewery. Since prohibition has become
an imminent menace among the English-speaking
races, beer has taken a new place in the affections of
mankind, and the man who is thirsty feels himself
an idealist as his grandfather never did in the same
circumstances. Hence an attack on a brewery is
likely to be a more passionate affair than an attack
on a mineral-water factory. It will surprise nobody
to be told that in the affair round the Montreal
brewery "many lost their hats and had their clothing
torn in the rush."

It is extraordinary to what an expense of time
and money people will go in order to get something
for nothing. A hat costs a great deal more than a
bottle of beer, yet here apparently were men who
counted their hats well lost if only they could get
a bottle of beer without paying for it. A suit of

clothes, again, would keep a man in drink for several weeks; yet there were men in Montreal who would rather risk the ruin of their clothes than miss the chance of a free bottle of beer. I doubt if it is the price of the bottle of beer of which they are thinking, or if they would allow their clothes to be torn in a street tussle for the sake of eightpence or so. There is something in human nature that takes an unaccountable pleasure in getting things for nothing apart altogether from their value. Perhaps it is a part of every man's dream of the perfect world. There are no shops in fairyland; at least, if there are, there is nothing to pay. You go into them and order what you like, and it is all sent home to you for nothing. William Morris conceived a world of this kind in *News from Nowhere*. But the notion of gratis shopping never caught on as it deserved—perhaps because Morris did not make the people in his shops give away the right things. At the same time, people will undoubtedly accept for nothing even things that they do not much like. Consider how many people will go and sit through a bad play merely because they have been given free seats. If for some reason they are unable to go themselves, they will take the greatest pains to persuade others to fill their places. "It's a pity to waste them," they say, as though it were not a great deal better to waste a complimentary ticket than to waste an evening. It is all very well to say that you should not look a gift-horse in the mouth. But there are many horses that I for one would not take

as a gift, and I have no desire to receive for nothing
an animal that I would count dear at ten shillings.
In this, I know, I am a little less than human. The
experience of the human race is against me. "You
can have it for nix," said the man in the Southend
hotel about the ticket for the performance of "Daredevil Dorothy"; and his friend did not even trouble
to ask him whether "Daredevil Dorothy" was a
good play—as from its name I have no doubt that
it was—so pleased he was at getting the ticket "for
nix." There are occasions, however, when even getting things "for nix" is no consolation. For instance,
I have a friend who was doing some work in connec-
tion with the Wembley Exhibition and whose work
took him into the stall of a celebrated whiskey firm.
The man looking after the stall asked him to "have
something," and my friend agreed that he would.
"Have a drop of our liqueur whiskey," said the
other—"pre-war; it's a treat." "Right," said my
friend, and his face shone as he watched a large
glass of the precious fluid being poured out, coloured
like the sun, and mixed with a gush of soda. He
did not taste it for some time, but went on with his
work, thinking how pleasant it was to get liqueur
whiskey for nothing and enjoying it drop by drop
in his imagination in advance. At last he took up
the glass, gazed at it lovingly for a moment and put
it to his lips. What was his astonishment to find
that it had no taste whatever—that, at least, it had
no more taste than a tumbler of soda-water. He
began to wonder whether it could be that this

famous firm of distillers made a whiskey so mild that
its flavour could not be detected in a glass of soda-
water. He took another sip, and again failed to
discover the least trace of the flavour usually asso-
ciated with whiskey. He looked round for the head
of the stall, but not being able to see him, called to
his assistant and asked him if he would mind tasting
the whiskey to see if it was all right. The assistant
did so, put it down hurriedly with a wry face, and
exclaimed, "My God, he has given you dummy!"
The head of the stall was immediately sent for, and
asked out of what bottle he had taken the whiskey.
He produced a bottle that was more than half-
empty and that turned out to have no smell and to
contain nothing but coloured water. The head of
the stall began to tear his hair. "Oh Lord," he
groaned, "there were all sorts of important people
here yesterday—let me think for a minute—there
was Sir John This and General That and Admiral
the Other—and I gave them all dummy and told
them how good it was. What on earth can they
have thought? And none of them said a word!"
It may be that Sir John This and General That were
so human that, in their pleasure at being given
whiskey for nothing, they did not even notice the
remarkable fact that it had no taste. On the other
hand, I suspect that each of them, having been
brought up on that pernicious proverb about not
looking a gift-horse in the mouth, were inhibited by
shame from pointing out to their host that, doubt-
less through inadvertence, he was inviting them to

drink coloured water. It speaks volumes for the
politeness of the island races that K.B.E. and Admiral alike had swallowed their doses like men or,
perhaps, had furtively poured them into flower-pots
like men. Not always, however, have Englishmen
behaved with such self-control, as Dickens makes
clear in that scene in which Uncle Pumblechook
drinks the brandy that Pip has unknowingly diluted
with tar-water. Uncle Pumblechook, you will remember, overlooking the fact that he was getting the
brandy for nothing, behaved in the most unmannerly
fashion, leaping into the air and making faces and
comporting himself like a mad creature. How much
superior is the modern man with his sense of obliga-
tion to the man who is giving him something for
nix!

The love of something for nothing, however, had
probably become a great deal more wide-spread since
Dickens's day. Nowadays we even expect to be insured for nothing by our morning paper, and Mr.
Shaw is probably only a little in advance of the modern spirit when he demands that we should not
merely be given railway travel for nothing, but that
we should actually be paid a bonus of twopence a
mile for our trouble. In the age of Dickens scarcely
anything was free except salvation. I remember
hearing a noted evangelist of the Victorian Age
reading out that beautiful verse from Isaiah: "Ho,
everyone that thirsteth, come ye to the waters; and
he that hath no money, come ye, buy and eat; yea,
come, buy wine and milk without money, and with-

out price," and how, at the end of the verse, he paused and: looking morosely at the congregation, observed, "Here's a chance for a Scotchman!" I doubt, however, if the Scots are ahead of the other civilized races in this love of getting something without paying for it. The ancient Romans, as they became more civilized, grew more and more notorious for their passion for free bread and circuses, and it is probable that the hatred of paying bills, which is only another form of the love of getting something for nothing, is a characteristic of every advanced civilization. That is why the advanced civilizations ultimately fail. They do not like paying their bills, and yet they cannot devise a social system such as Morris dreamed of in which the payment of bills has become unnecessary. Morris' prophecy, however, remains a truthful picture of the perfect world, and idealists will not lightly abandon their dream of a State, in which we shall all live in charming houses for nothing, and eat charming food and drink charming wine for nothing, and go on our travels for nothing, just as we are already insured for nothing. The Montreal mob that stormed the brewery was merely registering the eternal human protest against the evil custom of having to pay for things. In spirit most of us were with them. I cannot pity a man who lost his hat in so good a cause.

## What Katy Did at School

I T is probable—nay, certain—that, while nearly
all girls read their brothers' books, very few
boys read their sisters' books. I am not sure that
until this year of grace, I had ever read a girls'
book through. It would have seemed an abdication
of manhood, when I was a small child, to sit down
seriously to *Queechy* or *Little Women,* or *Daisy in
the Field.* I could sit enraptured while a great-aunt
told me the plot of any of these stories in her own
words, and I still seem to remember an incident
from a book called *Melbourne House,* in which a
little girl asked to be allowed to become a com-
municant before the usual age for doing so and,
after much discouragement on the part of her elders,
had her claim admitted. I may be confusing *Melbourne House* with some other book, but the little
girl's faith in contrast to the worldliness of some of
her elders made a profound impression on me. If
I avoided girls' books, indeed, it was not because I
had an ultra-virile contempt for goodness. So far
as I can remember, I always liked other people to
be good. I can even now see in my mind's eye a
front page of the *Band of Hope Review,* containing
a picture of a young sailor saying his prayers before
turning in for the night, while the other sailors
jeered and threw pillows at him. It was called "He

Stands Fire!" and was an illustration to a story in which the young sailor of the picture wore down the levity of his messmates by his nightly persistency in prayer till at last one of them said: "He stands fire, boys. Let him alone." I enjoyed dozens of stories of the same kind in a book called *Bible Models*. It was a book of sermons, in which a judicious child could ignore the theology and concentrate on the anecdotes. It was there that I first read the story of the sentry who stood at his post while the rocks from the volcano kept tumbling down on him. That is how I liked human beings to behave. It would have been impossible to be too virtuous to please me at the age of seven. In later life we make a joke of the boy who stood on the burning deck, and we should deplore it if at a crisis our own children behaved with similar stubbornness, but I had no scruples in my admiration of the little fellow then. You had only to be a martyr in those days to make me your slave. If you gave your life for somebody else, or were burned at the stake, or were tied to a post and left to be drowned by the incoming tide, or were sent to jail for reading the Bible, I would follow you loyally to your doom in my imagination. Even in books of modern life my heart was all with the slum-child who was beaten for refusing to assist in a burglary at his father's bidding. I fancy stories of good children who disobeyed their wicked parents were fairly common in the nineteenth century. It was a strange paradox that, in an age that set parents on a pedestal, re-

ligious literature should have been so lavish of
parents who were monsters of wickedness. There
were not many bad mothers in the stories, but bad
fathers were almost universal. There was a narrative poem that moved me deeply about a dying child
with a drunken father. Lines such as "Father, dear
father, the clock has struck one," and "Father, dear
father, come home," still touch me when I remember them. Never in vain in those days did an author
invite my pity with a scene in which the wicked
parent stood by the death-bed of his virtuous child
and saw the error of his ways. Even to-day I am
not sure that these things are not truer to the essen-
tial facts of life than a great deal of the realistic
and psychological fiction of the last half-century.
At least, they would be truer if extremely wicked
fathers with extremely evangelical children were
commoner than they are. But alas! in my own experience, I have known more families in which extremely evangelical fathers had extremely wicked
children.

Comparatively little of my reading, however,
even at an early date, consisted of pious fiction.
This was chiefly reserved for Sundays, when Kingston and Ballantyne and Edwin S. Ellis became
pagan authors, and *Wops the Waif* or *No Gains
Without Pains* suited better with the atmosphere
of the day. On weekdays I think I preferred a Red
Indian brave even to a burglar's son who in order to
escape parental violence had to go to Sunday school
in secret, and my ordinary heroes were men who

suffered at the hands of Barbary pirates rather than
at the hands of their fellow-Christians. I had a
moderate taste for blood, and liked my young hero
none the worse if he could wield a cutlass to effect
among a mob of savages. Children are very exact-
ing in regard to their heroes. They maroon them
on desert islands; they cast them alone on the sea in
open boats and let them all but die of thirst before
a lucky shower of rain falls and makes a pool of
water in the spread-out sail; they subject them to
mutiny, to irons, to the bastinado; they lose them
in the jungle, with jaguars crouching in wait for
them in the branches of trees; they bring them
within range of the Red Indian's scalping-knife; they
make them a butt for poisoned arrows. In all these
things, it may be, they are simply telling the same
story as that copy of the *Band of Hope Review*—
the story of a youth who stands fire. It is one of
the universal stories; it is as old as the story of
Ulysses. Ulysses, no doubt, would make a dubious
hero for a serial in the *Band of Hope Review;* but
like the boy who said his prayers, he fascinates us
in his capacity of "the much-enduring." All great
fiction is a moral tale, even though it succeeds in
hiding its moral from those who would not like it.
I was astonished lately, on reading one or two books
by Ballantyne and Kingston, to find how overwhelm-
ingly moral the adventure stories of my own childhood must have been. As a child I could so shut
my eyes and ears to sermons and pass on from them
to the serious business of the anecdote that I seldom

noticed I was being preached at, and, if I did, I would forgive the parson for the sake of the pirate. But, when I read *Martin Rattler* aloud to my niece, as she lay ill, she cried out in distress alike at the stretches of sermonizing and at the stretches of scenery. She is one of those children who not only can endure, but insist upon, being read to for hours at a time when they are ill. But the pious interruptions of Ballantyne had such an effect on her, and wrung such sighs and moans of protest from her, that I had to go out to a bookshop and look for something less likely to raise an already risen temperature. That was how I came to read *What Katy Did at School*.

Having read it, I do not feel that I lost very much by never reading girls' books when I was young. *What Katy Did at School* is, apparently, a classic of its kind, and is republished year after year in different editions by different publishers, but I honestly believe there is less in it to stir the pulses than in any school-story I ever read. It does not contain a single fight; it does not contain a single football match. The most thrilling scenes in the book occur as the result of one of the schoolgirls writing a letter to a boy in which she says: "If I let down a string, would you tie a cake to it, like that kind which you threw to Mary Andrews last term? Tie two cakes, please; one for me, and one for my room-mate" and signing Katy's name to the letter. The letter, as you may guess, is discovered by a schoolmistress, and Katy protests her innocence in vain. It is all the harder on Katy because she is really the best girl in the school and has formed the other good girls (including the mischievous good girl) into the S.S.U.C. (or Society for the Suppression of Unladylike Conduct), with a constitution the first article of which runs: "The object of this Society is twofold: it combines having a good time with the pursuit of VIRTUE." Katy, alas! has far from a good time. She is almost expelled, and is doomed to spend the rest of the story in heaping coals of fire on the head of the mistress who wronged her and on that of the wretched little glutton, Bella, who had forged the name of Katy Carr. Poor Bella, she had wanted a cake so badly! Her confession of her sin to Katy is disarming. "Berry Searles doesn't care a bit for us little girls," she says to Katy, "only for big ones. And I knew if I said 'Bella,' he'd never give me the cake. So I said 'Miss Carr' instead." Whereupon Katy forgives her, and even I find myself softening to her. In the story of Katy, as in the *Odyssey* and in *He Stands Fire,* we see the appeal of the much-enduring. And that may be why thousands of little girls still read *What Katy Did at School.* Or, perhaps, they read it only because their elderly relations insist on presenting them with it. At the same time, in spite of an occasional groan, readers of *What Katy Did at School,* if they are never entirely interested, are never entirely bored. Besides the "much-enduring" motive, they have the "mischievous angel" motive, and **Rosamund Redding, called Rose Red** for short

by her friends, must reconcile many children who
would otherwise find the good example of Katy
rather overpowering. Few of us can resist the fascination of mischief combined with virtue, such as
Rose Red's. Even so pious an author as Miss Susan
Coolidge was obviously attracted by the notion of a
girl who was at once as mischievous as the bad girls,
and as virtuous as the good ones. It is a mixture
rare in life but irresistible when it occurs. Mr. Kipling gave us a mixture of much the same kind in
*Stalky and Co.*—schoolboys who were honourable
lawbreakers, scamps of whom the angels would not
disapprove too strongly. What charms us in characters of this kind is that they carry their virtue so
easily. We like to see virtue moving through life
with as free a gait as vice; and, indeed, it is doubtful
whether the bold, bad men of fiction would interest
the world as they do if it were not for this air of
freedom with which they are invested and for the
fact that so many of the virtuous characters seem
to be so unbending in their excellence. But there
is no use in trying to be mischievously virtuous unless you are born to it. If you do, you will only
achieve an offensive vivacity. Rose Red was mischievous virtue natural and predestined. If ever I
read *What Katy Did at School* again—which I
won't—it will be for her sake.

## Revels

HE was undoubtedly a man who liked to see other people happy. I am not sure that he ever smiled himself, but he was always organizing amusements for "the young of all ages." Sometimes he let off fireworks in the evening; once he brightened a grey afternoon by letting off daylight fireworks which, as they exploded, released charming little parachutes in the French national colours or tiny airships carrying the French flag. He was himself a Frenchman, big, heavy, and serious. He always wore a *béret* in the hotel, and, as he sat at a corner table in the dining-room among his friends, it seemed to set him apart like a crown, and, indeed, to ennoble him into a kind of king of the bourgeois. His friends all talked at the same time, and waved their hands at the same time, and were perpetually laughing. But he sat among them, silent, grave, and without a gesture. If the waitress was slow in serving him and his friends, he would give the table three sharp and regal raps, but that was as far as he ever went in the outward display of emotion. But all of us who were staying at the Hotel de la Bouteille at Grandepluieville came to regard him with the tenderest sentiments, and to say to each other such things as that he had a good heart, and that he was fond of children. When a notice was

put up in the hall of the hotel announcing that a
*bal costumé* would take place on Saturday, and that
everybody who wanted coloured paper for fancy
dresses could obtain a supply of it for nothing at
the bureau, we all knew at once that it was only the
good heart of M. Tel that could have planned such
a thing. Every child in the hotel that was able to
walk without help was immediately in a dance of
excitement, pleading to be allowed to stay up late
for so great an occasion. It is usually easy for a
child to persuade a French or an Irish parent to
allow it to sit up till midnight, but English parents,
misled by a jingle about the virtues of earliness in
all things, are less amenable to reason. Still, as a
result of coaxing, threats, and the absurd hold that
the young have on the affections of their elders,
every child in the end obtained the desired permis-
sion. Even parents who could not themselves be
present allowed their families to sit up in the care
of responsible persons, so that I, for example, found
myself cast for the part of father to no fewer than
three families.

We were a rather excited collection as we
crowded into the dining-room for dinner on Saturday evening. We three families had a large round
table to ourselves—Charles dressed as a pirate with
a skull and crossbones on his black paper cap and a
long wooden sword at his side, Ronald disguised as
a rabbit with a furry headpiece that could be pushed
back when he wanted to eat, Peter dressed as some
kind of nobleman in a yellow paper hat and a purple

paper gown, and all the girls rustling in coloured
paper dresses and looking like the most luxurious
kind of Christmas crackers. As the different guests
came in, dressed as gipsies, Italian village girls,
married peasants with imitation babies, and looking
like the company in a music-hall revue, the other
guests clapped them loudly, and, when the applause
was subsiding, a Frenchman would cry out: *"Un—
deux—trois,"* and we would pay them a tribute in
the manner of Kentish fire. Then a huge man came
in wearing the white cap and costume of a chef. He
wore a mask over the top half of his face—a mask
rather like the top half of the face of Mr. Chester-
ton—and carried a large basket over his arm. The
forks and spoons tinkled on the tables under the
vehement reception we gave him, for everybody
knew that this was M. Tel of the good heart. Then
*"un—deux—trois,"* and we cheered him uproar-
iously again. He went slowly round the tables with
his basket, leaving on each handfuls of little
coloured balls for throwing at people and rolls of
coloured paper for hurling in streamers across the
room. The children wished to begin throwing
things at once, but in response to an earnest appeal,
they consented to wait. Charles, meanwhile, was
stretching across the table and trying to put the
point of his sword into my eye in order to attract
my attention, and obtain my ruling on the question
whether it would be all right to begin throwing
things after the soup was finished. I could see that
a mutiny was brewing, for even the girls were grow-

ing restive and their hands were playing nervously
with the little coloured balls that lay so temptingly
at the sides of their plates. But I still counselled
patience, and, when Hélène brought the soup, I felt
that now peace was secure for at least three minutes.
Unfortunately, a guest at some other table took
advantage of our preoccupation with the soup to
hurl a streamer among us. This was more than
Peter, who was sitting opposite me, could stand.
He rose in his place, and, with the force of David
aiming at Goliath, flung a blue ball which struck me
under the eye and fell with a gentle splash into my
soup. I must say Peter was quite nice about it.
"Sorry," he said; "I was trying to hit that bald man
at the far end of the room." Then Charles, not
to be outdone, rose in his place, and with equal fury
threw a pink ball which hit me just over the eye and
also fell into my soup-plate, where it floated prettily
beside the other one. "Sorry," he said; "I was
aiming at the red-haired girl sitting beside the window." By this time the battle was joined all over
the room, and missiles were falling through the air
like a storm of hail. It was impossible to eat a
spoonful of soup without getting a crack on the ear
or on the back of the neck. I do not know whether
Charles and Peter hit me again, because I was hit
so often and from so many sides that I lost all power
of spotting the aggressor. Streamers were by now
festooning the room. They were hanging in scores
from every gas-bracket within an inch of the uncov-
ered flames till strong men anxiously cried out that

the place would be set on fire, and that, as the walls were of matchboard and many of the dresses of paper, none of us would be able to escape. I kept my eye on a possible exit through an open window, and tried to remind myself: "Women and children first." All the same I fancy I should have made an effort to get through the window before Peter and Charles. The streamers were now lying in a thick tangle across our and everybody else's table. They were round our necks. They were trailing in the soup. They were trailing in the butter. In order to get a spoonful of soup to your lips you had to pass it deftly through hole after hole in the many-coloured net, and then you were lucky if you did not find yourself swallowing a repulsive blue ball. Then Hélène came to clear away the soup-plates, and, as she took them up, the soup-soaked streamers slid off them and left soupy and buttery trails on one's trousers and sleeves and shoulders. My dinner-jacket is not a very expensive one. Still, if I had foreseen that streamers would be thrown during the soup, I think I should have come to dinner in a bathing-costume. The children in the meantime had retrieved most of the balls that had fallen into the soup and were storing them up on the table as reserves of ammunition. I insisted that they must at least be wiped dry before being thrown, but, after somebody had hit me with a wet ball on the right cheek, I ceased to care, and even tried to incite a small girl of another man's family to dip her roll in her glass of Evian and throw it at a clergyman.

By the time the chicken was served there was no unused ammunition left. A girl from a neighbouring table crept up behind Ronald (who, you may remember, was disguised as a rabbit), with a lettuce-leaf that was squelchy with oil and vinegar and crushed it through the open rabbit's mouth on the top of his head. "Bunny must be hungry," she said gently; "bunny must have some dinner." And she thrusts the unseemly vegetable still further in his hair. Many of the children, in the meanwhile, were on all fours under the tables collecting the balls that had fallen and renewing the battle as soon as they had enough of them. M. Tel sat phlegmatically at his table in his chef's costume, occasionally aiming a pellet at the back of a lady's head and then looking away suddenly with an air at once of innocence and of sadness. If a child approached him to throw things at him, he did not smile but opened his mouth gravely so that the child might try to hurl a ball into it. He sometimes took a stroll round the room, lowering his head and opening his mouth as he passed a child and never smiling. I have no doubt he was in the seventh heaven of happiness. And so were Charles and Peter. Charles had by now lost his pirate's cap and his sword was on the floor, but he was running about the room with sweat-soaked hair and taking cover behind chairs as he pelted the auburn-haired lady and dodged her return missiles. Peter had also sought out an enemy of his own and was carrying on a private war at the far end of the room. As for Ronald, he was content to hop up and

down with hands pendent and say that he was a
rabbit. I asked Hélène to bring me a liqueur
brandy. . . .

In time the dinner came to an end and with it, the
battle. The tables were cleared away, and the
chairs arranged in rows, for some of the French
guests were about to give us a revue—*La Revue de
Grandepluieville*. I intended to write a description
of this entertainment for women and children, but it
is impossible. The first scene I did not understand,
but I laughed when I heard other people laughing,
as one usually does at a foreign play. I could see
that the plot had something to do with visitors arriving at the Hotel de la Bouteille and asking for
accommodation. One of the actresses was even
made up as a travesty of the landlady of the hotel.
The scene over, somebody called for *"un—deux—
trois,"* and we gave them with a will. The next
scene appeared to represent two guests in pyjamas
wandering about the corridor of the hotel at night
with candles in their hands and fighting as to which
of them should enter a room first. The word
*cabinet* recurred again and again, and at last one of
the men took down a time-table from the door of
the room, and told the other that no one was allowed
to go in for longer than three minutes, and that each
guest was allowed to enter only during the three
minutes specially reserved for him. He then read
out a long list of names: "From midnight till three
minutes past, M. Blanc; from three minutes past to
six minutes past, Mme. Blanc; from six minutes till

nine minutes past, Mlle. Blanc," amid shrieks
of laughter, giving, I fancy, real names, and
adding a few touches meant to appeal to
the English comic sense, such as: "From four
o'clock to three minutes past, Roojarde Keepling;
from three minutes past to six minutes past, Shairr-
luck Ums." The other guest pointed out that on
the previous day one man had occupied the room
for half an hour. "Ah, yes," replied the other, "he
is a poet and must have somewhere to write verses."
Another person who had occupied the room for an
unduly long time was also excused on the ground
that he wanted a place *"pour manger les petites
galettes."* Meanwhile, as each name was read out
from the list, the excluded guest would ejaculate:
*"Oh, ce cochon!"* or some equally opprobrious re-
mark. Finally the man with the list sang a song;
it was all about *cabinets*—the *cabinets* at the Hotel
de la Bouteille—and the scene ended with a dance
of the two pyjama-clad men with candles held high,
both of them singing a chorus about *cabinets*. I
fancy the song sung by a lady in blue glasses in the
next scene had the same subject, and I suspect the
parts I could not understand in the poem recited by
the little man with streaks of oiled hair crossing
his bald patch—a poem beginning:

Mangeurs et buveurs sans vergogne.

After that a Frenchman with a Marcel wave in his
red hair came out and sang a song in English. It
began to the tune of "Tipperary":

Eet's a lung vay to Grandepluieville,
 Ze sweetest spot I know.
Tank you for leaving Eastbourne and Bornmut,
 And coming uvver here;
If you vant ze French girls to lak you,
 Joost dreenk two bawttles of champagne.
Eet's a lung vay to ze peace of Europe,
 Bot ve're still friends, aren't ve?

When it was all over and the children sent to bed, and I went into the hall to look for Hélène and order a restorative, I ran into the bald little man with the streaks of hair across his skull. I shook hands with him, thanked him for his entertainment and asked him who had written the revue. "*C'est moi,*" he said, bowing in modest pride. I shook hands with him again in warm congratulation. "*Très bon,*" I said to him, enthusiastically, "*très*"— and I hesitated for the right word—"*spirituel.*" He bowed low, his face wreathed in happy smiles, and passed back into the dining-room where the first fox-trot was now in full swing.

## Animals in England

THERE have been men who hated their fellow men, but there have been few human beings even of this sort who did not in some degree like animals. The animal story is a favourite among primitive peoples, and, as children, we are universally attracted by stories in which animals are among the characters. The history of our race begins almost with the appearance of an animal who exercised such a fascination over our first parents that the world has never been quite the same since. There was Noah in his floating Zoo at the second great crisis in human history. And, all through the long narrative, the animal is a continual intervener —the lion that Samson slew, the bears that punished the children who exclaimed (as well-behaved children wouldn't have done) that Elisha was bald, the ass of Balaam—and the very shapes of animals cast a spell over certain passages in literature, sacred and profane, as when we read about the worship of the Golden Calf or about the wooden horse that bore stealthy ruin into Troy. In the nursery we loved even animals that we had never seen— or loved to read about them—the lion and the unicorn, the fox that ate the grapes, the dragon, and the wolf that dressed himself up as Red Riding

Hood's grandmother. Robert Bruce and Little Miss Muffit lived in our minds almost entirely because of their association with spiders. Even Dr. Watts was memorable because he wrote not only of doing good but of dogs and of bees. There are people who talk as though the feeling for animals were a disease of the modern imagination, and as though in the more heroic records of mankind no one ever took any interest in a bird or a beast except with a view to killing it. The chief difference between modern man and his ancestors in the feeling for animals, it seems to me, is that those of us who live in towns nowadays are not living in a populous world of animals as our great-grandfathers did; they were interested in animals because they saw them every day, while we are all the more interested in animals because they have so decreased in comparison with ourselves that we have to make an effort and deliberately go out to see them. We are also, and for much the same reasons of scarcity, sorrier for animals than our ancestors were, and we therefore attribute rights to them and are more disturbed if they are cruelly treated. But the interest of the human imagination in animals was just as great in the days when men wrote such stories as that of Jonah and the whale as it is in the age of *The Bad Child's Book of Beasts* and *The Jungle Books*.

Hence, when a child is taken to the Zoo, or a cattle show, or a horse-race, it probably feels much the same kind of excitement that was felt during his childhood at the spectacle of living creatures by the author of the *Book of Genesis*. And at a cattle show or at a horse-race we are all children. All, perhaps, except a few experts. They are experts who do not understand why ordinary human beings should care for horses, cows, sheep and pigs. They see an animal as a congregation of points—good and bad—and their chief pleasure lies in judging it and in putting it in their minds against other animals for appraisement. Most of us, however, when we see an animal, admire it without any desire for settling its place in the hierarchy of its rivals. If we admire a Shire stallion or a Shorthorn bull, we are as uncritically excited by it as by the sight of a mole or a hedgehog. Who, on seeing a mole tearing at the earth in order to escape from our presence, would dream of comparing it for width of shoulders or length of snout with other moles? It is for us simply a mole and indistinguishable from any other mole. In the same way, if we see a parade of Shire stallions at a show, we do not trouble ourselves about those points that enable judges to place one before another in order of merit. If we prefer one to another, it will more probably be because of its colour or a white star on its forehead than for any reason that would weigh with the censor. Hence an ignorant man may be as happy at a horse show or cattle show in his own fashion as a farmer.

We who are ignorant, it seems to me, would do well to attend these shows assiduously just now, for if we live to be old men and women, we shall be

able to tell the children of a wonderless age about
the wonders of a world that has vanished. Those
who were fortunate enough to be present at the
Royal Show at Leicester, I am sure, were spectators
of a very beautiful England that is quickly passing.
Every year the display of machines at agricultural
shows becomes proportionately greater, and, just as
the roads are being more and more given up to machines, so are the shows and the fields. The horse
is on his last legs, except as an aid to amusement,
and, when Mr. Henry Ford has achieved his dream
of taking the burden of drudgery off flesh and blood,
and transferring it to machines, that poor drudge,
the horse, is unlikely to be kept save as a pet. I
should myself, I confess, like to see Shires and
Clydesdales used in a new sort of polo. They would
be slower than polo-ponies, but how magnificently
they would gallop through the game! These huge
and hairy-footed beasts have a martial air as they
canter loose about a field that would look positively
noble if good riders were on their backs. Or we
might have special races for them at race-meetings.
A Derby of Suffolk Punches would be sufficiently exciting, and there is no reason why we should confine
contests of speed to the swiftest breeds of horses.
It is the contest that is exciting in these matters, as
is manifest from the fact that, even in an age of
aeroplanes, we are still carried out of ourselves by
the spectacle of a neck-and-neck race between Mas-
sine and Filibert de Savoie for the Gold Cup at
Ascot. Why, if speed were everything, we would

have a man on a motor-bicycle who would beat both of them.

It has certainly been a melancholy thought, ever since the first invention of the motor-car, that the world was bound to become less and less like the circus we always loved, and more and more like the factory we always hated, but we have only to look at the streets of London to realize that our gloomiest anticipations have already come true. We have sacrificed that honest drudge, the horse, and what have we got for it but a block of motor-buses in the Strand? Already many people are putting the blame for the congestion of traffic on the few horses that remain, and are declaring that no horses should be allowed in the streets of London. This, no doubt, will come in time, but, in fairness to the horses, I should like to see another law made that no motor-cars should be allowed in the country. If townsmen have such an itch for movement by machinery, let them confine their vice to the cities and leave us the country that we knew when we were children and Lofty was a foal. Zoölogists have recently been writing to the *Times* about the need for the preservation of gorillas in Africa. How much more urgent is the need for preserving horses in England! In another generation, if you wish to see a horse in London, you will have to go to a race-meeting or the Zoölogical Gardens. If only the recipe for machines could be lost, like the recipe for Robots, how quickly the roads of London would become beautiful again! But soon there will be no animals left in cities, except cats and sparrows and houseflies. It now seems almost certain that the housefly will survive the horse. What a comment on what a world!

But an agricultural show such as that at Leicester is interesting to most of us, even apart from the fact that it is an exhibition of vanishing animals. However accustomed we are to the sight of bulls and horses and pigs and sheep, the bulls and horses and pigs and sheep that we see at a great show are as different from them as are the peas that we see in a seedsman's catalogue from the peas in our own garden. Everyone who has ever attempted to grow vegetables knows how even the most expensive seeds refuse to produce those prodigies of the photographs in the catalogues. He cannot grow those nonpareil peas himself, nor does the greengrocer ever send them to him. Yet somehow, somewhen, somewhere, someone has grown them, or they would not be in the photographs; and if he goes to a horticultural show, there they are, larger than life, carrying off the prizes. At the Royal Show, the horses and pigs are larger than life; the bulls and sheep are larger than life. There is something even alarming in proximity to such monsters, and I confess when a Large Black boar, great as an elephant, with tusks and frothing chaps, came grunting towards me over the grass, my instinct was for flight. Instinct is a good guide. I fled.

Not that I dislike pigs; I always had a peculiar affection for them. How often as a child I have hung over a piggery door gazing with satisfaction at a foul and sleeping beauty at peace in the straw! Especially delightful to the eye is a young family of pigs. They are among the most taking of Nature's decorations. They are so comical in their little sudden frisks, in their little curly tails, in their squeaky, quarrelsome voices. "This little pig went to market. . . ." Only a race that loved pigs could have invented the nursery patter. I prefer to think that it was into little pigs of this kind that Circe turned the companions of Ulysses. If it was into the Large Black boars of a rural show, the story becomes hideous. For a Large Black boar is a mass of all the ugliness that might well have made St. George himself quake with fear, and St. George was a brave man. The Large Black boar is an exaggeration of evil, a knock-kneed embodiment of sloth and gluttony. He is a beastly Falstaff without a smile. I never believed the evil that men speak of pigs till I saw the boars at Leicester. If the other animals were also exaggerations, and were monstrosities rather than creatures one would expect to meet on a farm, they were at least splendid in excess —bulls as prodigious as thunderstorms, rams in quest of which Jason might have voyaged to Colchis. They did not seem quite real, but they were legends for the memory. They bore the same relation to the animals of common life that heroic literature bears to the life you see in the Strand. The Zoo itself does not contain creatures more superb in captivity than the red bulls with terrible necks that marched slowly in procession round the judges at Leicester. As company, I prefer the calf, the lamb and the foal, but the bull in the show ring must be given the prize for the gorgeousness of power.

## Making the Most of Life

CHILDREN are a notably ambitious race but it is never easy to know, till he tells you, the ruling passion that glows in any particular child's breast. I heard a small boy of three being examined the other day by his inquisitive elders on his views with regard to his future. He was first asked whether he would like to remain at the age of three for ever or whether he would rather be grown up. He said: "Be grown up." He was then asked, after the fashion of those who have lost their childhood, why he wished to be grown up, and what he would do when he was grown up that he could not do already. He replied, almost without needing to pause: "Have a knife." His elders pressed him with the question, what he would do with the knife. "Cut things," he told them, smiling as if struck by a sudden thought; "cut butter."

Those of us who already possess knives and use them as a matter of course at our meals can hardly understand the longing of an infant to be given the freedom of so perilous an instrument. Man has been defined as a tool-using animal, and there is no other tool that appeals to the imagination of children so strongly as a knife. It is through long months and years a forbidden thing, and all the more fascinating on that account. There is no glory

in using a spoon, even though there should be an
apostle on the end of the handle. There is no
honour in holding a fork in the right hand and in
taking up on it little squares of meat that have been
cut with a knife by some more privileged hand.
Fork and spoon are little more than an extension
of the fingers, and a spoon, at least, is so safe that
it can be left in the hands of an infant in the cradle.
But a knife is a danger against which constant warning is necessary—something out of reach and waiting as a prize at the end of a long avenue of years.

It is characteristic of the emptiness of human
dreams that, though every child longs to have a
knife, he does not really desire it for any particular
purpose. The boy who said that he wanted a knife
in order to cut butter was, I am sure, guilty of an
evasion. He had to justify his longing for a knife
with some reason or other, and it may be that he
thought that if his parents could be persuaded he
wished only to cut butter with it, there was more
chance of their letting him have one early. But
no child cares a bad farthing about cutting butter.
He longs to use a knife with a sharp edge—the sort
of knife that could cut bread and meat, and sharpen
pencils and even cut sticks out of a hedge—the sort
of knife that, if it slips, draws blood—the sort of
knife that has something of the dangerousness of a
weapon. Hence his boundless pride in being given
his first pen-knife. It is difficult for those of us
who are no longer children to believe that happiness
can be substantially increased by the possession of

a pen-knife. If we were asked to name the things that make life most worth living, none of us would think of putting a pen-knife even at the foot of the longest catalogue. A pen-knife, at the best, is a convenience. If it is blunt, it is a nuisance. But we never dream of regarding it either as an exciting treasure or as a badge of manhood. Now that we are able to sharpen our own pencils, we feel no happier than we felt before. We have the power to cut sticks out of hedges and to carve our names in the bark of trees, but it no longer gives us any pleasure to do so. Yet time was when the human being we envied most was the boy who on his birthday had been given a bigger pen-knife than any of the other boys possessed. Do they still make such monstrous knives nowadays—knives that contain not only large and small blades, but a pair of scissors and a corkscrew and a hook for picking stones out of the feet of horses? With the disappearance of the horse, the instrument for removing stones from horses' feet will probably also disappear, and there may even be a movement among optimists to prevent so sinister an instrument as a corkscrew from being placed in the hands of little children. But the chief glory of the knife—its sharp, shining blades—will still remain, inciting children to live dangerously, and providing them with a weapon as efficient as the claws of a tiger or the teeth of a lion.

We regard children with condescending amusement, because so little a thing as a knife makes them so happy. But I wonder whether, if it were not for the necessity of making a living, nine-tenths of those of us who are middle-aged would be doing many more useful things than cutting our names on the bark of trees. Every day, we see or read about people who can afford to amuse themselves without working, and their amusements are as a rule just as childish as those of a small boy with a knife in a garden. If I imagine myself a millionaire, I usually imagine myself doing nothing, or at least, doing nothing that would be of any use to anybody. Sometimes my dream of great riches becomes touched with morality, and I have thoughts of putting a part of my million to noble uses. But I am afraid that, if I possessed it, the first thing I should do would be to cease working and to go and live in Italy, where I should idle away month after month amid a cloud of good intentions for the future. I doubt if I should do anything much more useful than cutting butter. I should like to be rich, but I scarcely know why I wish to be rich, except in order to escape being poor. The pleasures of the rich are, in practice, extraordinarily limited. They can wear more and better clothes. They can eat more and better food, and drink more and better wine. They can afford to play baccarat instead of boule at the casino. They can travel first class and stay at the best hotels. They can parade the lawns in the Royal Enclosure at Ascot and in the Royal Yacht Squadron at Cowes. They can ride and sail and kill birds. They can sit in a box at the opera. Moralists tell us, however, that all these things do

not bring happiness, and that indeed, they are no
more to be taken seriously than the small boy's
pride in his pen-knife. It is questionable whether
the pleasure of having a knife is not really superior
to all the pleasures that afterwards take its place.
If only we could go on enjoying it in later life, we
could dispense with most of these other pleasures.
What greater satisfaction of one's vanity is there
to be had, for instance, than from carving one's
name on a tree? There you make your mark on the
world. You leave a lasting record of your initials.
There is pleasure, too, in eating through the bark
and in exposing the glistening wood of the tree. If
we could go on being happy doing this sort of thing,
there would be no need of drinking or playing
bridge. Nor should we need to go out to the
Amusements Park at Wembley and pay huge
machines shillings and sixpences for hurling and
tossing us about like flotsam on a rough sea. The
grown-up world, it seems to me, has learned how
to work, but it has not learned how to amuse itself.
If it had, all the most melancholy literature would
not have been written by men who had amused themselves with the completest indifference to the con-
sequences.

I am not enough of a pessimist to believe that a
world which contains friendship, books, music,
churches, seas like peacocks, Sussex, gardens, willow-
wrens, rivers, children, and dinner-tables surrounded
by wits, is all dust and ashes. But the Amusements
Park at Wembley does make one wonder whether

children are not, after all, a little wiser in their pleasures than their elders. I confess I am prejudiced against Wembley because I got into one of the amusement contrivances by mistake. I thought, when I paid my sixpence at the gate of Over the Falls, that I was going to sit in a boat and glide over a gentle slope and visit illuminated caves. I was all the more surprised, on entering, to find myself in a dark passage, walking along a ricketty floor that seemed to imitate an earthquake under my feet and to be meant to shake me into a state of terror. At the end of the passage an attendant thrust me into a lift and told me to sit down. "Now for the boat," I said to myself, expecting to be lowered gently to the edge of the water. What was my horror, however, to find the far side of the lift suddenly disappearing, the seat collapsing under me, myself flung on my back on the floor, and precipitated at an immense speed down a steep place, bumped, banged and breathless, whither I knew not and was too startled to care. There was nothing to do but to lie on one's back with one's boots in the air and pray till it was over. I was too much surprised even to feel afraid. I imagine death must be something like this—the released spirit borne whizzing along a passage with a stream of light at the end, only half-conscious of its position, too terribly amazed to be able to wonder either what has happened or what is happening. My faculties were too badly scattered to notice so much as that there was a crowd of sight-seers at the end of that rum-

bling Niagara of wood that bore me along. The
sight of me may have interested them. The sight
of them did not, at that desperate moment, interest
me. The worst of it was that, thinking only of
the illuminated caves, I had persuaded two ladies,
to say nothing of two men of delicate sensibilities,
to accompany me into the extraordinary machine.
It was an amusement to which I would not have
introduced my dearest enemy. A soldier of the
Great War told me that he could not remember
having had quite such an experience even in the
trenches. Yet we who laugh at small boys for want-
ing pen-knives with gimlets or corkscrews, actually
pay money in order to be tossed about on these
wooden tides of torture.

Life, it seems to me, is worth living, but only if
we avoid the amusements of grown-up people. Few
of us, unfortunately, have the courage to refrain.
We stand outside the Caterpillar or the Whip, and
someone says: "Be a man!" and in a moment we
are in our places and are being thrown about like
pieces of a star not yet formed but whirling through
chaos. It is a challenge to the semi-lunatic in each
of us. Alas! the child with the pen-knife is a philosopher in comparison. He is learning to be a
man. We, for our part, are not even learning
to be children. We are simply killing time by
methods that look like a harebrained attempt to
kill ourselves.

## Bond Street

THE shopkeepers are carrying on an agitation against the motor-bus—or, at least, against the excess of motor-buses—in Bond Street. They feel that the street is being ruined—that it is no longer a paradise of shoppers, but that it is rapidly becoming as noisy and as common as Oxford Street. Shoppers, they think, are being frightened away by these great penny vulgarians, which get in the way of motor-cars and make it impossible to cross the street except with the aid of a policeman. They dream of a Bond Street that will be a worthy resort of wealth and leisure—a Bond Street in which it will be easy to forget that anybody was ever poor or economical, and that, life being what it is, the demand for coffins is still more pressing than the demand for pearls. Their Bond Street would be a charming way of the rich, as remote as Bath from the rumour of the general struggle for cheap joints and cheap beer. It would tell the world of a settled civilization, in which no price was too high to pay when luxury was at stake. Here, and in the by-ways leading from it, the whole world would expose its costliest merchandise, and jewels and clothes and pictures would be even more beautiful than the money or the bright eyes of those who purchased them.

I cannot with a good conscience blame the Bond Street shopkeepers or join with those who denounce them for impudence, greed, and snobbery. I, too, once dreamed of a perfect Bond Street. Not that I wished—or, at least, hoped—ever to shop in it, but that I liked to think of its being there. That was before I had ever visited London, when the names of London streets—the Strand, Bow Street, Threadneedle Street, Piccadilly, Baker Street, Finchley Road and Bond Street—were known to me only from books and newspapers. But the names of the streets gave me pleasure as names like Ispahan and Trebizond give pleasure to romantic people, and I thought of them as the map of a thousand marvels. If I admired the West End of London in anticipation, it was, I fancy, not because I believed it to be full of rich people but because I believed it to be full of Greek-godlike people who were rich enough to afford a proper setting for their Greek-godhead. That, I am sure, is the explanation of the customary spell that dukes and other aristocrats in novelettes cast on simple minds. It is not that the simple minds are worshippers of rank and wealth, but that they have a generous hope that somewhere on earth there exists a race of human beings of extraordinary beauty, noble in the very carriage of their bodies, with characters to match, fearless, imperturbable, incapable of dishonour even if capable of evil, and with every physical circumstance favouring them. I did not expect to find exactly that kind of semi-divine person com-

ing out of the shops in Bond Street, perhaps, but
I had some hopes of a superabundance of loveliness.
I think I expected to see men and women walking
up and down Bond Street at least like handsome
actors and actresses, and looking as if they had
been trained by Sir Frank Benson. No doubt, there
would be ugly and comic characters, but the dominant
figures in the scene would be men and women—
especially women—who might conceivably have
stepped out of the leading parts in a novel or a
play.

There is great pleasure in admiring other people,
and, if you admire them, you would like them to
live in unintermitted sunshine, whether in a garden
or on a sea-front or in a street full of shining carriage wheels. This, also, I think, is comparable to
the passion of the theatre. You demand consummate-
ness not only in the actors but in the scenery.
Hence, in the perfect Bond Street it was always
May and June—the May and June not of the
weather reports, but of fiction. Life as it was carried on there never ceased to reflect the brightest
of the stars. Pain and poverty were exiled. The
human beings, though noble enough to have preserved impavid countenances had the heavens fallen
on them, were, in plain fact, untouched and un-
threatened by disaster, and, if they confronted danger, it was only for love of it. You may think
that it was a materialistic dream, but then, if I had
been a mystic, I should not have idealized Bond
Street. There were, concurrently with this, cold-

bath periods when hardship and self-denial seemed better than happiness, but, on the whole, I liked the thought of money, extravagance, and the life of those who toil not, neither do they spin, and are charming in their idleness more than I liked the life I was living myself. I am not sure that I ever wished to own a carriage and pair, my ambition not rising above jaunting cars, polo-carts, gigs, croydons, or, at most, a phaeton and a pony, but I liked the spectacle of men and women being borne along behind two noble horses, with a coachman and a groom doing their best to look nobler than the horses. What more golden throne has there ever been for human beings than a carriage and pair?

And now that is all past. Or, if such a carriage survives here and there, it seems but a faded relic and an anachronism. The wheels do not glitter as they used to glitter. The whole affair looks slow and incompetent, and we wonder that we could ever have thought it so fine.

But it may be that the illusion of Bond Street had vanished even before the appearance of ten thousand motor-cars. It did not, I suspect, survive the first visit to the enchanted pavements. There is no use in idealizing human beings in advance. They are not a godlike race. Even in seasons in which they dress as the sons and daughters of God ought to dress—and this occurs but seldom—they are in the mass a disappointment to the romantic spirit. The rich have their own peculiar charm, but Apollo and Venus have never been common figures

in any street in any city. I doubt if the faces in
Bond Street are any more beautiful than the faces
in Camden Town, and great possessions do not
ensure even a graceful figure. There is most prettiness, perhaps, where there is most wealth, but, if
there is, it is for the most part the result of artifice.
Extreme beauty or even extreme prettiness is as rare
almost as genius, and you might spend a week in
Bond Street without being startled into admiration
of either of them. It would not be fair to blame
Bond Street for this. A street full of wonderful
human beings has no more place in reality than has
an eighteenth-century pastoral. Indeed, it is open
to doubt whether even one absolutely beautiful person has ever existed except in the imagination of
someone who has abjured experience for fairyland.

We can recover our early illusions about human
beings to some extent in the theatre; at least, we
could until the footlights began to be done away
with. It is easy to believe that an actress is more
beautiful than she really is. Or, at least, it was a
few years ago. The limelight pleads for her.
Every circumstance except her photograph pleads
for her. We go into the theatre in a deliberate
spirit of make-believe and give our imaginations a
license that we do not allow them in the street. This
is certainly true of some of us. There are others,
happier still, who can visit any famous place in
the same mood in which we go to a theatre. They
see what they expect to see. They are never disappointed because all the world's a stage to them,

and they carry about with them wherever they go the fantastic light that makes all things beautiful. But this power of self-deception is not universal. There are people who see geese as swans, but even with them it is usually only a few geese of their own, not the whole tribe of geese. Most men at an early age lose faith in the very existence of a general Arcadia of either rural or urban beauty. So desperately do some of them recant that they will even contend that Mr. Bateman is the supreme realist of our time in his drawings of men and women. Unless I am mistaken, Mr. Lucas once declared that Mr. George Morrow was the most truthful living delineator of the modern Londoner. If this is so, it is clear that youthful idealists who expect to find figures worthy of the cadences of blank verse flitting through the sunlight of Bond Street are doomed to disappointment.

I cannot then feel so strongly as I once might have done about the throng and the tumult of motor-buses in Bond Street. If I like Bond Street now it is because it is the street in which you can buy pianola-rolls and gramophone records, and because there is a shop in it which sells the perfection of cream cheeses. There is also a money-lender in it who frequently attempts to thrust large sums of money on me and who will not accept the snub of my silence. But, apart from these things, I doubt if it is either a very interesting or a very beautiful street. I don't think that it matters to anybody except the shopkeepers whether motor-buses are allowed in it or not. I should, of course, like—at least, part of me would like—to see motor-buses banished from all the streets of London, and horses coming back, and the hand of progress stayed. But I find motor-buses more of a nuisance in the Strand and in Fleet Street than in Bond Street, and I see no reason why Bond Street should be favoured above these. Is a Bond Street money-lender better than any other money-lender, or is afternoon tea in Bond Street better than afternoon tea in Glasgow? I wish the world contained even one street in which everything in the shops was better than could be found in any other street, and in which the spectacle of the stir of life came up to the dreams of the writers of novelettes. But, if such a street exists, I do not think that it is called Bond Street.

## Bed-Knobs

"**D**O you need bed-knobs, scissors . . . ?" I forget how the rest of the notice ran—I saw it only for an instant above a shop from the top of a bus in Camden Town. Scissors, of course, everybody needs, but has Camden Town really such an appetite for bed-knobs as would justify this order of precedence in an ironmonger's advertisement? I send down a hook to the bottom of my memory, but I cannot recall a single occasion on which I needed a bed-knob so desperately as to go out and buy one. And yet the question, "Do you need bed-knobs?" seems curiously inviting. Perhaps the children of the Camden Town streets find it irresistible, for children have always been fascinated by bed-knobs. It is possible that some of them, more imaginative than the rest, having sixpence to spend, will lay it out on a bright gold bed-knob even in preference to brandy balls or liquorice laces or whatever the young eat nowadays. The nineteenth century has many sins to answer for, but children should always hold it in grateful remembrance as the century which filled the world with iron bedsteads, decorated at the four corners with brass knobs. There is on general grounds, I agree, little to be said for iron bedsteads, but is the modern return to wood in the bedroom, pleasant though it is to the eye, quite fair to the rising generation? There is an extraordinary satisfaction to be got under the age of ten from unscrewing a knob from the foot of the bed and screwing it on again. It is a satisfaction that lasts many years after the child has ceased to take any interest in seeing whether it can get its toe into its mouth. The game of twisting back the leg till the toe reaches the mouth is a good game in its season, especially if played against a rival, but its joys are manifestly fleeting and of brief date. Bed-knobs remain, when one has put away and almost forgotten such childish pleasures, as something for which it is worth waking up in the morning. Even before one got up and dressed it was a temptation to slide down to the foot of the bed and to begin screwing the knobs off. (Surely, by the way, there should be some worthier name for those globes of gold that, like Matthew, Mark, Luke and John, guarded the four corners of one's infant slumbers.) One's bed might have either round knobs or tall, grooved, quasi-conical knobs. The grooved knob was more interesting in itself and in the oddity of its shape, but the round knob was on the whole to be preferred, for it was not only a knob but a mirror. You could look at yourself in it as in a mirror, as you can look at yourself in a spoon or a silver teapot. Bed-knobs, spoons and teapots, it seems to me, are the most desirable of all kinds of mirror for the young, because they encourage curiosity rather than vanity. You are not tempted to admire yourself in the back of a spoon. That lean face narrowing at one end to a still leaner and cretinous brow, that bulbous projection of nose, that body far too tiny for so large-nosed and elongated a countenance—these are no flatterers. Bring your face nearer the spoon, and your nose swells beyond Disraeli's—nay, beyond Cyrano's. Luckily for your peace of mind, when you are a child it never enters your head to say to yourself: "Suppose that is what I really look like. Suppose it is the back of the spoon, and not the mirror, that tells me the truth. Suppose that is how the angels see me." The experience of the eye, no doubt, confirms the report of the mirror against that of the spoon. But who knows for certain that the eye is not a deceiver, leading us to folly and destruction? Had Narcissus but looked at himself in the back of a spoon instead of in the pool, he might have been a wiser and a sadder man. And I am not sure that, in real life, the back of the spoon does not reflect Narcissus more accurately than the beguiling water.

Even if you look at yourself in the inside of a spoon, you will see nothing that is likely to make you faint with admiration of so nonpareil a beauty. Rather, you will be filled with the delicious amazement that comes of seeing your image suspended upside down. The world is full of a number of things, but few of them have given pleasure to a greater multitude of human beings than this. It projects you into a world that laughs at reality like the world you read about in *Jack and the Bean-*

*stalk.* Men of science may have a reasonable explanation of the inverted image in the hollow of a spoon. I neither know, nor admit it. I am content to look on the matter as a mystery of nature requiring no explanation, like the shape of a flatfish. Turn the spoon upside down, turn it sideways, and still the image hangs head downwards. Let us not try to rationalize miracles. If we understood all that we see in the hollow of a spoon, we should understand everything, and the human mind is not meant for that. Teapots are, it may be, less mysterious than spoons, but they have the advantage that they introduce us to a larger and more varied spectacle. Man, looking into a spoon, is an egotist —a disappointed egotist, no doubt, but still a self-regarding and self-scrutinizing creature. The world is hidden from him by his own image, and even the room in which he sits scarcely exists for him as he gazes on his eyebrows, his nose and his mouth, and turns them this way and that for a more curious view. In the round silver teapot, however, the walls of the room become real to him, hung with even tinier and more charming pictures than any that were painted for the Queen's Dolls' House. He sees, too, the images of other people, and cups, and chairs, and the toast-rack, and books, and the bowl of flowers. He sees the firelight dancing and lighting up a room prettier than the crookedest room in the little crooked house of the nursery rhyme. It is true that, by putting his face near the teapot, he is again brought up against the vision of the extravagant nose that he had seen in the spoon, and that the smallest child in the world can make its hand seem the largest thing in existence by advancing it towards the silver bulge of the pot. These, however, are mere moments of egotism in an interest that embraces every minutest detail among the things reflected. In the teapot the ego can escape from its prison and take a light-hearted and objective view of things. That, I fancy, is the second secret of happiness.

It is one of the distinctions of bed-knobs that in their manner of reflecting the outside world they effect a reasonable compromise between the egotism of the back of the spoon and the altruism of the teapot. I speak from memory on this matter—I have searched the house in which I live for a bed-knob in order to put it to the test, and have searched, alas, in vain—but I am almost certain that in a perfect bed-knob one can see one's own face and at the same time get a sufficient glimpse of the world in general. A tiny wash-hand-stand and a tiny towel-rail, a tiny coal-scuttle and a tinier kitten, are visible in the distance in that brilliant sphere. One can look into it and see the nurse getting smaller as she draws near a diminutive cupboard and takes out of it a tea-canister so small that it would be lost in the hollow of a fairy's thimble. It was in the gleaming round of a bed-knob, I fancy, that Mr. de la Mare first saw the Midget.

And yet I doubt if our love of bed-knobs had at first much to do with the mysterious life that goes

on in the heart of the little brass planet from the
first raising of the blind. We loved bed-knobs
chiefly because we could unscrew them. We made
the attempt with feeble fingers when it was still a
Herculean task. And then one day the knob began
to move, slowly, and turn by turn, till suddenly it
was free in the hand, leaving the screw discrowned
and naked. Strange to say, the screw, lacking
though it was either in the beauties that charm the
eye or in those that warm the heart, never disappointed us. For all its uncomeliness, it had at least
one unending excellence: it was something on to
which you could screw a bed-knob. It is true that
you did not always screw on the bed-knob very skil-
fully. Sometimes it got a twist that set it a-tilt
on its eminence like a drunkard's hat. This was
especially often the case when you had been unscrewing it and screwing it for years, and the thread of
the screw got worn or the inside of the knob had
lost its power to grip. Children, indeed, are rough
in their methods, and have little mercy on such
things as bed-knobs. They experiment. They wish
to find out whether the knob at the right hand of
the bottom of the bed will fit the screw at the left
hand of the bottom of the bed, and whether the
smaller knobs at the foot of the bed will fit the
screws at the top. This is bad for bed-knobs, and
accounts for the battered expression that they wear
as they rest at uneasy angles. What I never could
make out, however, was how bed-knobs got lost.
Children might leave them lying on the floor; they

might even use them as appurtenances of a game and mislay them amid the ragged chaos of their toys. But no child ever threw a bed-knob out of the window, and there is no other exit save the door. It is hardly conceivable that even the most careless servant could sweep up so obvious a utility into the dip of her dust-pan. Yet how else did the knob from the left-hand bottom corner of my bed disappear? Week after week, month after month, it had fallen again and again from its worn-out screw at a touch. Then, I suppose, someone got tired of hearing it fall, and, instead of putting it back, placed it on the mantelpiece where it would be beyond accident. Then someone else, weary of the sight of so unbecoming an ornament on the mantelpiece, threw it into a drawer or cast it on a heap of broken things for the dust-bin. Whatever may have been its fate, I woke up every morning for years into a ruined world in which one of the first sights that met my eyes was that forlorn and widowed screw. You may think that the absence of a single bed-knob would make little difference to the appearance of a room, but in point of fact it made the whole room look awry, producing as disastrous an effect as would the absence of a tie in a man in evening dress. It may be that Camden Town is fuller than most places of homes in which such mysterious disappearances have taken place, and that tidy householders do consequently need bed-knobs in such quantities as to give them a value above scissors in the hardware shops. Or, perhaps, it is the children who insist on having the four corners of their beds restored after loss with each golden ball complete. Children are pampered nowadays.

Pampered though they may be, however, I do not envy those of them who sleep in wooden beds. That child alone is to be envied who sleeps in an iron bed with not only a knob at each corner, but with numbers of other little knobs, golden and globular satellites of the great knobs, perching on every bar. How does a modern child, sleeping in a wooden bed, contrive to get through the day without weariness? It is bound to get into mischief with its idle hands. The child, on the other hand, who lives in a house that is full of beds with brass knobs has always something to do, and for such a child Satan spreads his net in vain.

(1)

**THE END**